Miami
Past & Present

Donald D. Spencer

Schiffer Publishing Ltd
4880 Lower Valley Road Atglen, Pennsylvania 19310

Dedication

To my brother and his wife,
Bob and Shirley Spencer

Other Schiffer Books by the Author:
A History of the Alligator: Florida's Favorite Reptile, 978-0-7643-3083-4, $24.99
Greetings from Orland & Winter Park, Florida: 1902-1950, 978-0-7643-2966-1, $24.99
St. Augustine, Florida: Past and Present, 978-0-7643-3146-6, $24.99
Greetings from St. Augustine, 978-0-7643-2802-2, $24.95
Greetings from Tampa, Florida, 978-0-7643-2898-5, $24.95
Greetings from Sarasota, Florida: Bradenton & Surrounding Communities, 978-0-7643-3213-5, $24.99
St. John's River: An Illustrated History, 978-0-7643-2826-8, $24.99
Greetings from Jacksonville, Florida, 978-0-7643-2958-6, $24.99
Greetings from Ormond Beach, Florida, 978-0-7643-2809-1, $24.95
Daytona Bike Week, 978-0-7643-2977-7, $24.99
Greetings from Daytona Beach, 978-0-7643-2806-0, $24.95
Greetings from Palm Beach, Florida: 1900s-1960s, 978-0-7643-3263-0, $24.99
'50s Roadside Florida, 978-0-7643-3364-4, $24.99
Greetings from Fort Myers & Sanibel Island, 978-0-7643-3305-7, $24.99
Mid-Century Vegas: 1930s-1960s, 978-0-7643-3129-9, $39.99

**Unless otherwise noted, all images are the property of the author.*
Library of Congress Control Number: 2010940204

Cover and book designed by: Bruce Waters
Type set in Souvenir Lt BT

ISBN: 978-0-7643-3623-2
Printed in China

Schiffer Books are available at special discounts for bulk purchases for sales promotions or premiums. Special editions, including personalized covers, corporate imprints, and excerpts can be created in large quantities for special needs. For more information contact the publisher:

Published by Schiffer Publishing Ltd.
4880 Lower Valley Road
Atglen, PA 19310
Phone: (610) 593-1777; Fax: (610) 593-2002
E-mail: Info@schifferbooks.com

For the largest selection of fine reference books on this and related subjects, please visit our web site at:
www.schifferbooks.com
We are always looking for people to write books on new and related subjects. If you have an idea for a book please contact us at the above address.

This book may be purchased from the publisher.
Include $5.00 for shipping.
Please try your bookstore first.
You may write for a free catalog.

In Europe, Schiffer books are distributed by
Bushwood Books
6 Marksbury Ave.
Kew Gardens
Surrey TW9 4JF England
Phone: 44 (0) 20 8392 8585; Fax: 44 (0) 20 8392 9876
E-mail: info@bushwoodbooks.co.uk
Website: www.bushwoodbooks.co.uk

Donald Spencer's postcard and photograph collection form the base for this book, augmented by photographs from the Florida State Archives Photograph Collection: 12 (lower bottom), 16 (top), 17 (right top), 30 (left top), 61, (LB), 73 (lower bottom), 80 (lower bottom), 87 (lower bottom), 121 (top).

Contents

Preface

The realities of the past are swept away by time, but the essence of the past is still approachable in old postcards and photographs. Such is the case in this treasury of vintage postcards of Greater Miami contrasted with contemporary photographs, many of which are taken from the same vantage point.

The old postcard views were carefully selected for historic relevance from the author's postcard collection. The author then photographed the same sites enabling viewers to witness the forces of change and evolution in the city that is often called "The Magic City."

Included in this archive of evocative images are such historic landmarks as Miami News Tower, City Hall, Fort Dallas, Post Office, Olympic Theater, County Courthouse, as well as side-by-side views of Flagler Street, Biscayne Boulevard, South Beach's Ocean Drive, Bayfront Park, Lummus Park, Cape Florida Lighthouse, and Miami's sparkling skyline.

Extensive captions by the author, accompany the postcards and photographs, offering historical background, anecdotes and detail about the site or locale depicted. Also included is an informative Introduction, outlining Miami's role as the "Crossroads of the Americas," Cruise Capital of the World, and the center of international trade and commerce, and the use of postcards in preserving the city's past.

Miami Past & Present is the story of Miami and its people and how they have molded this beautiful and picturesque place into one of the most visually exciting cities in the world. The 337 postcards and photograph views in this book document the growth of Miami from the early days of ancient Indians through the present.

Part I:
Introduction

Chapter One:
Florida's Early Years

The First Residents

Life in what is now Florida was quite different when the early Indian civilizations lived here. What we know about these people comes from studying artifacts — the man-made remains such as tools, weapons, clothing, skeletons, and bits of pottery. Archaeologists study artifacts and interpret clues about the way prehistoric people obtained food, how they ate, how they built houses, how they dressed, how they worshipped and how they battled enemy tribes.

The Indians of Florida probably came across a land bridge that once connected Asia to Alaska, over what is now the Bering Strait. They may have followed animals southward, and slowly over thousands of years ventured into the area we know as Florida. They were all Mongoloid peoples and we refer to them as Paleo Indians, meaning old or ancient Indians.

The Paleo Indians killed mastodons, saber-toothed tigers, and other large animals. The Paleo hunters used stone-tipped spears to kill some of them and stampeded others into traps.

Most of the Paleo Indians became hunter-cultivators with strong family and tribal ties. They were all similar in appearance with bronze skin, strong arms and legs, wide skulls, high cheekbones and straight black hair.

Indians in the Archaic Periods that followed were less dependent on large animals. They killed small animals with darts and spears and gathered the produce of the land and sea.

The early Indians were hunters and nomadic wanderers. When they arrived at the St. Johns River around 5,000 B.C. they found enough food to remain in one area. They began constructing shelters for protection from the more dangerous animals. They found fallen trees and hollowed them out for dugout canoes. This allowed them to travel greater distances, faster. It helped spread their culture throughout the area.

The early Indians learned to use flint and make simple pottery. They learned that maize (corn) placed in the ground would grow more maize. This discovery changed these Indians from hunters to farmers. Now they could establish permanent villages.

A society began to develop as stronger men became chiefs and their children were prepared to succeed them. The growth of villages developed into tribes and families stayed together longer. This gave them protection. Sometime during the development of the tribes and villages, religion began to develop.

The Florida Indians built houses of materials found near their villages. The Indians in central and northern Florida were forest people. They had homes of wooden poles and logs, with roofs of grass or palm fronds. The Indians of southern Florida had few trees in their areas. They built their homes of mud and sand, with roofs of palmetto fronds.

In 1500, there were probably more than 100,000 Indians in Florida and people from Europe began coming to Florida. At this time the four major Indian groups or tribes were the Timucua, who lived in the northeast; the Tequesta, in the southeast; the Calusa, in the southwest; and the Apalachee, in the northwest Gulf region.

Early Indian Hunters. Paleo Indians killed mastodons and other large animals for food.

Discovering Florida

One of the companions to Columbus on his second voyage was Juan Ponce de Leon, a Spanish explorer and as brave a soldier as any of that band who came over the great ocean in search of adventure. Instead of returning to Spain, he remained at Hispaniola (today this is Haiti and the Dominican Republic). He conquered the island of Porto Rico (today this is Puerto Rico) for Spain. In 1513, he outfitted three small vessels and, while cruising among the Bahamas Islands, he sighted land on Easter Sunday, March 27. After coasting along the shore for several days, he landed and gave the name Florida to the country. He raised a cross and planted the Spanish flag, thus taking possession for the Spanish crown.

The Discovery of Florida. On March 27, 1513, Easter Sunday, Spanish explorer, Juan Ponce de Leon and his three ships — the *Santiago*, the *San Cristobel*, and the *Santa Maria De La Consolacion* — sighted an island and continued north until they anchored offshore on April 2nd and came ashore on April 3rd. He thought he had discovered an island, which he named Florida, the flower. Instead of an island, Ponce de Leon had landed on the east coast in what would become central Florida.

Tequesta Indians

Five centuries ago Miami and Key Biscayne were the realm of the Tequesta Indians, a people whose ancestors had lived in the region for thousands of years. They plied the waters of Biscayne Bay in dugout canoes, traveling back and forth among their villages and fishing and shellfish-gathering camps. Apparently the Tequestas liked this area and remains of what may be their largest village sites have been found here.

Where today there are hotels and other buildings at the mouth of the Miami River, there was a major Tequesta Indian village. When late nineteenth century settlers founded Miami, hundreds of shell and earth middens and

Prehistoric People in South Florida. More than 4,000 years ago Native Indians occupied the area on both sides of the mouth of the Miami River, where it met Biscayne Bay. In 1513, Spanish explorers encountered these Tequesta Indians and wrote about the lifestyles of Miami's first residents. Miami's first people traded with other prehistoric people in Southwest Florida, North Florida and Georgia. This view appears at the Historical Museum of Southern Florida.

burial mounds left behind by the Tequesta and their ancestors blanketed both banks of the Miami River near Brickell Point, the banks of Key Biscayne north of the Cape Florida Lighthouse, on Miami Beach, along Little River (present-day Fort Lauderdale), and other sites in the region. Before Miami was Miami, it was Tequesta Indian country.

The boundaries of the Tequesta Indians probably occupied most of present Miami-Dade County and may have lived a far north as Pompano Beach in Broward County. To the west and south, their lands merged with those of the Calusa Indians. Exact lines may have wavered from time to time as the more powerful Calusa dominated Tequesta settlements. The same situation has been considered likely for the Florida Keys.

The Tequesta Indians preferred living near the mouths of rivers, on inlets, and along the coastal beaches. Many of the beaches were separated from the mainland. The Tequesta lived a wholesome outdoor life, had much exercise in the Florida tropical air, and ate a varied diet of palmetto berries, coca plums, sea grapes, prickly pears, wild figs, seeds, nuts, wild grapes, huckleberries, bear, deer, wild boar meat, turtle meat, and lots of fish such as sailfish, sting rays, porpoises, sharks, many small fish and manatees. In the winter all the Tequesta Indians would go in the waters of Biscayne Bay in their canoes to hunt for manatees, or sea cows. The manatee was considered a delicacy and served mainly to the chiefs and other prominent leaders.

The Miami River yielded gar, sunfish, and bowfin. Biscayne Bay gave the Tequesta Indians large quantities of snapper, toadfish, turtles and catfish. The shallow ocean beyond Key Biscayne produced barracuda, grunt, grouper and jack. But the big prizes were the sharks, manatee and whales, found both in the bay and in the ocean.

The Tequesta used shells and shark's teeth for various tools, including spearheads, hammers, fishhooks, drinking cups, and chisels. Shark's teeth were also used to carve out logs to make dugout canoes.

Many ceremonies were held at a special place on the opposite side of the Miami River from their village. The Tequesta knew it as the house of spirits; today it is called the Miami Circle. Ancestors of the Tequesta had built the structure many years ago, and it had been maintained ever since. It was the people's most important structure and was the spiritual center of the community.

The Tequesta made flour by grinding the roots of the coontie plant. Unfortunately, many food sources were not very plentiful in the Biscayne Bay area, so the Tequesta never became a large or powerful tribe compared to their western neighbors, the Calusa Indians. It is estimated the Tequesta numbered about 800 and the Calusa around 2,000.

The Tequesta Indian tribe and its chief were held in high status by the powerful Calusa Indian chief in southeast Florida. This alliance was in part cemented by marriages among high-ranking families.

Tequesta Indian Society. Centuries before Columbus set foot in the Americas, a highly developed Indian civilization was flourishing along the grassy marshes of Southeast Florida. These direct descendants of Florida's early mastodon hunters were given the name Tequesta by the first Spanish explorers. By the beginning of the sixteenth century, the Tequesta Indians controlled the southeastern area of Florida. This view appears at the Historical Museum of Southern Florida.

Spanish Soldiers Explore Tequesta Country

In 1513, Spanish explorer Juan Ponce de Leon, after landing on the central east coast and claiming the land for Spain, sailed south and anchored his ships in Biscayne Bay. A shipwrecked Spanish sailor later named that bay in honor of his native Bay of Biscay in northern Spain. Ponce probably visited the Tequesta Indian Village that stood on the north bank where the Miami River flushes into Biscayne Bay. The village was called Chequescha and was the first recorded place named in Southeast Florida. Later, Spanish explorers called this place Tequesta in honor of its chief. The chief lorded over a territory that covered present-day Miami-Dade County and up to the Broward County area. Our scant facts about the Tequesta come solely from two hundred years of slanted Spanish writings and from sparse residue left by the Tequesta.

On Ponce de Leon's second journey to Florida in 1521, he sailed to the southwest coast of Florida, around today's Charlotte Harbor, a deep-water port. Soon after his arrival, Juan was felled by an arrow from a Calusa Indian. The expedition immediately withdrew and set sail for Puerto Rico, where Ponce de Leon died.

In 1567, a Jesuit, Brother Francisco Villareal, established the first mission near the Tequesta village on the Miami River. The Indians helped him to erect a large cross and to build twenty-eight simple houses within a stockade. However, discontent among the Spanish soldiers stationed there due to the sand flies, mosquitoes, boredom and the long, hot summer led the thirty garrison soldiers to harass the Indians and brought abandonment to the mission. The mission was reestablished the following year, however, it lasted only another two years. The Tequesta Indians were not good converts to Christianity.

The Spanish attempted to establish another mission in 1743; however, it was also ill-fated. It lasted only six months. Florida became a British possession in 1763 and the Spanish and several Tequesta Indians who feared the British would take them for slaves, departed for Cuba.

The Tequestas Disappeared

By the late 1700s, most of the Tequesta Indians had succumbed to European-introduced diseases for which they had no immunity, including chickenpox, measles, and smallpox. The Spanish had enslaved some Indians while others died in warfare. The Tequesta Indian's last major activity was a mass evacuation of the Miami area. Many of them went into the Everglades; others moved to Cuba.

Spanish Explorers Land in South Florida. Spanish soldiers arrived at the Tequesta Indian village on the north bank of the Miami River. This 1973 postcard of a painting by Ken Hughes shows an artist's reconstruction of the first recorded European contact in the Greater Miami area, commissioned by the Historical Museum of Southern Florida.

The Seminole Indians

On the heels of the vanishing Tequesta and Calusa Indians came the Seminole Indians from the north. They came in groups between 1750 and 1809. The Seminole's accepted into their fellowship runaway slaves from southern plantations and stray Indians from other tribes. They refused to give up these slaves and strays, even at the order of plantation owners or of the United States Government.

Many of the Seminole Indians lived in the Everglades area west of Miami, consistently refusing to become part of any community life except their own. They poled their dugout canoes in and out of winding waterways, hunting and fishing, and keeping as far from the white man and civilization as they could. Their fathers had little cause to trust the word of their conquerors.

U.S. Gains Possession of Florida

Spain was unable to control the Indians and rule her territory. Finally, after much discussion, a treaty was signed in which Spain agreed to transfer Florida to the United States for the sum of five million dollars, and the payment of certain claims. The exchange of flags took place on July 10, 1821, at St. Augustine (capital of East Florida), and on July 17, 1821, at Pensacola (capital of West Florida). After more than three hundred years of Spanish and British rule, Florida became part of the United States. In 1822, the United States made Florida a Territory. It then began to prepare Florida for statehood.

The Seminole Wars

The three Seminole Indian wars were brought on by U.S. territorial expansion, native factions resisting the U.S. policy of removal, and slavery. There was a constant turmoil on the Florida border. Slaves seeking freedom slipped across from Georgia and Alabama. Parties of slave catchers roved in Spanish North Florida. The Spanish government could not maintain order.

During the Seminole Wars of 1817-1818 (First Seminole War) and 1835-1842 (Second Seminole War), Florida became saturated with forts, camps, stockades, and blockhouses of all descriptions. During this period more than eighty forts were in use throughout Florida. Fort Dallas (now downtown Miami) and Fort Bankhead (now Key Biscayne) were two of these forts.

Florida Becomes A State

In 1838, Floridians held a convention for the purpose of writing a constitution or a set of laws by which the state would be governed. Fifty-six people from all parts of the territory took part in this convention. Florida voters approved the constitution in 1839 and six years later Florida became the twenty-seventh state in the United States.

Seminole Indians. The Seminole Indians found in Florida today are descendants of the Creeks and other closely allied tribes who united with fugitive African American slaves from the early English and Spanish colonies, and driven southward by warfare, eventually absorbed the straggling Indian groups that remained in South Florida. These Indians live in the southern part of the peninsula.

Civil War (1861-1865)

The Civil War was a period of internal conflict for the United States. In 1861 Florida seceded from the Union and joined the newly formed country, the Confederate States of America. Also in 1861, the Civil War began between the United States of America and the Confederate States of America. The war between the North and South lasted four long years, 1861-1865. It was the most tragic war in American history. More Americans died in the War Between the States than in all wars of the United States combined, until the Vietnam War.

Americans Settle in Miami

In the aftermath of the Second Seminole War (1835-1842), few persons wanted to live in the area now known as Miami. To encourage migration to the area, the U.S. Congress passed the Armed Occupation Act of 1842. Under the terms of this act, some families acquired land along the Miami River and in other parts of today's Greater Miami area.

The most prominent settler of that era was William English. Along with his mother, he purchased the 640-acre tract on the north bank of the Miami River that his uncle had developed as a slave plantation. English also purchased additional property on the south bank of the river. English began to build the village of Miami on the south bank of the river and rebuilding the slave plantation on the north bank. In 1844, English modified the Fort Dallas stone barracks as slave quarters (this structure was located where the Hyatt Hotel is today and, in 1925, moved to Miami's Lummus Park). English later left to strike it rich in California's gold rush and was accidentally killed in 1856. In 1890, Julia Tuttle purchased English's property on the north shore of the river and, with assistance from railroad tycoon Henry M. Flagler, built the city of Miami.

Even before Julia Tuttle purchased this property in 1871, William and Mary Brickell and family purchased about 2,000 acres along the south bank at the Miami River's mouth where they operated a thriving Indian trading post. Seminole Indians, who lived just east of the Brickells in the Everglades, traded with them.

Chapter Two:

Greater Miami Area

The Greater Miami area comprises several communities, villages and municipalities, among them Downtown Miami, Miami Beach, South Beach, Coral Gables, North Miami, Little Haiti, Coconut Grove, Little Havana, North Miami Beach, Overtown, Liberty City, Hialeah, Opa-Locka, Miami Lakes, Bal Harbor, South Miami, Miami Shores, Sunny Isles Beach, Surfside, Key Biscayne, North Bay Village and Fisher Island.

Every neighborhood in the Greater Miami area has its own personality, culture, history, uniqueness, and stereotype; however, the common thread throughout the area is tropical surroundings — swaying palms, cool sea breezes, and sunshine.

Downtown Miami

Miami's downtown reflects the dynamic diversity that has made this town famous as the city of change. On July 28, 1896, the dreams of an industrialist and a visionary came to fruition; in a room above a pool hall on what later became South Miami Avenue, the City of Miami was born. It was the result of a deal made in October of the previous year between railroad businessman Henry M. Flagler and Julia Tuttle, known as the "Mother of Miami," a Cleveland widow who had moved to the area in 1890 after purchasing a large tract of land around the Miami River. After the hard freeze of 1894-95, which devastated the citrus crop in much of Florida, Tuttle sent Flagler some orange blossoms to prove that the Miami area had been unaffected. She offered Flagler half of her land holdings if he would bring his railroad to the area. Flagler brought his railroad, which was soon followed by hotels, businesses and hundreds of people looking for a new home on this tropical frontier. The incorporation of Miami was the start of a city that has preserved and prospered with an adaptability that has helped to make it one of the world's leading metropolitan centers.

Downtown Miami is home to a plethora of attractions that reflect the city's ability to look toward the future without losing site of the past. The Freedom Tower on Biscayne Boulevard is a monument to the city's ability to change. Originally built in 1924, it was the city's first skyscraper, has housed the offices of the *Miami News* and been the gateway to freedom for thousand of Cuban refugees. The ornate Gusman Center, originally built in the mid-1920s as the Olympia Theater, offers a wide selection of the performing arts, from stand-up comedians to the New World Symphony. The Miami-Dade Cultural Center, with its Mediterranean Plaza and cascading fountains, provides an Old World setting for Greater Miami's state-of-the-art public library along with a historical and fine-arts museum that often displays the works of world-renowned artists, past and present.

The Brickell Avenue area, just south of the Miami River, was originally the homestead of William Brickell, one of Greater Miami's founding fathers. The area has become an important part of Miami's business world — as well as its distinctive skyline. Many of the towering office buildings and residences that grace the Bayfront here have been internationally recognized for their innovative design.

Old Fort Dallas. Fort Dallas, built during the Second Seminole War (1835-1842) at the mouth of the Miami River, later became downtown Miami. This Alligator Border Postcard shows the officer's barrack building at Fort Dallas as it appeared in 1908.

Henry M. Flagler. In 1883, Henry Morrison Flagler, a retired Standard Oil Company executive, while visiting Florida on a holiday, realized that better transportation facilities were needed. From that point on, until his death in 1913, Flagler proceeded to help develop the East Coast of Florida. He built a railroad line, called the Florida East Coast Railway, from Jacksonville to Key West, and along the way he developed a number of grand hotels that catered to wealthy tourists. Shown is a statue of Flagler that stands in front of the Old Dade County Court House on Flagler Street.

Fort Dallas Park. Julia Tuttle's (founder of Miami) son, Harry, turned his mother's former home into a gambling casino called the Seminole Club; the spacious grounds around the home became a subdivision called Fort Dallas Park. A rock wall surrounded the park with rock columns marking the only entrance at the foot of today's S.E. 1st Avenue. Fort Dallas Park became an elegant subdivision near the heart of the city, home to many of Miami's more prominent families.

Elks Lodge. The Miami Elks Lodge moved into the building shown above in 1910. The Elks' building was located on the corner of 12th Street (later became Flagler Street) and Avenue A (later became Third Avenue). The building got a face-lift during the 1920s when its exterior was changed to the extravagant style that was popular at the time. Years later the Elks moved into a new lodge that was located on Brickell Avenue.

Miami City Hall. Built of native rock in 1909 as Miami's City Hall with an adjacent Fire Station building on the left. In 1928 the City Hall moved across the street to the then new 28-story Dade County Court House; this building became the Police Station. The structure was demolished in 1958 and replaced on the site by the Federal Building.

Monster of The Deep. Tourists boating on Biscayne Bay in 1908 said they saw a sea serpent with a body at least thirty feet in length. Famed Miami fishing guide Charles H. Thompson went in pursuit of this large sea creature. He never found it, but four years later, in June 1912, he hooked into a giant sea creature near Miami. Five harpoons, 151 bullets, and thirty-nine hours later he landed the 30,000-pound, 45-foot-long whale shark or Rhinodontypicus. It took the sea monster five days to die. The "Monster of The Deep" was mounted, exhibited at the Elser Pier, and later taken on a national tour.

Moonshining in Miami. Moonshiners were forced to run when authorities discovered a still on the edge of the Everglades, near Miami, in the late 1920s.

Hurricane in Miami. Hurricanes and Miami (as well as all Florida) go together like peanut butter and destructive jelly. On September 18, 1926, a West Indian hurricane struck Miami and the adjacent coast, wrecked ornate Venetian residences, hurled ships and yachts into the streets, left a trail of hundreds killed or injured and caused a property damage of $100 million. The above view shows a Flagler Street scene after the Miami hurricane.

Going to Sea. In the early 1900s steamships maintained regular schedules between Miami and Nassau, Cuba, and several Caribbean islands. These beautiful islands were world renowned as vacation paradises. Shown to the left of the ship and County Causeway (now MacArthur Causeway) are Palm and Hibiscus Islands. Miami Beach is in the background.

Ocean Steamship and County Causeway. In the 1920s, this three- and a half-mile causeway, now known as MacArthur Causeway, that connected Miami with Miami Beach had a two-way double automobile roadway and trolley tracks. This unusual feature of the channel running parallel with the causeway was of interest to the traveler who journeyed to Miami by steamship.

Streetcars in Miami. The streetcar was a common mode of travel in Miami and between Miami, Coral Gables, and Miami Beach in the 1930s. Shown is Trolley #231 of the Miami Beach Railway on exhibit at the Historical Museum of Southeast Florida in downtown Miami.

Miami-Dade Court House. When it replaced the original 1904 courthouse in 1928, this 360-foot high structure was the tallest building south of Washington, D.C. This neoclassical style, 28-story building once housed the city and county jails, which were stacked safely on the top nine floors. Each fall, turkey buzzards that migrated from Ohio took over the courthouse's ziggurat-stepped roof as their winter home. With the area a center of the downtown's civic and cultural life, this courthouse was for decades a landmark in Dade County (now Miami-Dade County), especially at night when the building was illuminated

Railroads in Miami. Henry B. Plant and Henry M. Flagler opened up Florida's railroad system in the late 1880s. By 1894, Flagler had extended his Florida East Coast Railway to West Palm Beach. When a severe freeze struck citrus groves the following year, Julia B. Tuttle, a large landowner in Miami, convinced Flagler to extend the railroad south of Palm Beach. As part of her campaign of persuasion, Mrs. Tuttle sent Flagler a bouquet of orange blossoms and foliage and even offered him a large tract of land in the present location of downtown Miami on which he constructed the Royal Palm Hotel. As compensation for linking Jacksonville to Miami in 1896, the railroad baron also received an incentive from the state: more than two million acres of land stretching the length of Florida's East Coast. Shown in the above postcard view is the *City of Miami*. This streamline train began service of December 18, 1940 with a seven-car consist and made the Chicago to Miami run in twenty-nine and a half hours. The colorful orange and green train left Chicago at 9:40 a.m. and arrived in Miami at 4:10 p.m. the next day.

Florida East Coast Railway Train. The Florida East Coast Railway fielded a brightly-colored fleet of passenger trains painted in red, yellow, and silver. These trains ran the length of Florida and hauled thousands of tourists to enjoy the warm weather and the ocean. Henry M. Flagler's Florida East Coast Railway reached Miami in April 1896. What a day that was! Pioneers from the Redlands, from Coconut Grove and from the Seminole Indians hunting grounds south of the Grove, came to Miami in sailing boats or followed the old trail through Brickell hammock to see the first wood-burning locomotive chug into Miami. In 1912 the Florida East Coast Railway gave Miami its longtime identifying name when they first referred to it as "the Magic City," a pseudonym that is still used today. Travel by train was by far the most popular way to reach Miami during the 1930s. Shown is the Florida East Coast Railway Streamliner *Champion* parked in downtown Miami. The Dade County Court House is in the background.

Fishing in Miami. Fishing and boating were important forms of recreation for Miamians and visitors alike in the 1930s and much of it revolved around Pier 5 in Bayfront Park. This view shows a day's catch for one fishing boat. Prize-winning sailfish like these test the skill of deep-sea anglers.

Miami Post Office. Architects Phineas Paist and Howard Steward designed the second Miami Post Office building, which opened July 1, 1933. The building, located at 300 Northeast 1st Avenue, used many native materials, including oolitic limestone (known as Key stone) for the exterior. The patio was ornamented with a volcanic stone found in Texas near the Mexican border; throughout the interior there were many types of marble. The structure cost approximately $2 million. More general delivery was handled here than in any post office in the country. The building served as Miami's principal Post Office until 1978. It is now a U.S. Federal Court House.

Orange Bowl Stadium. The Roddy Burdine Stadium (Orange Bowl) was the largest structure of its kind in the southeastern United States. The Stadium opened in 1935 and was double-decked in 1947. The stadium was named in honor of R. B. "Roddy" Burdine, pioneer merchant and one of Greater Miami's leading citizens. The annual Orange Bowl college football game was first held in 1935 at the stadium. For many years the University of Miami's Hurricanes football team and Miami Dolphins professional football team held their home games at the stadium. The Roddy Burdine Stadium, located at 501 Northwest Third Street, was demolished in 2008. Today, the Hurricanes and Dolphins play their home games at Pro Player Stadium, which is also the home of the Florida Marlins' baseball team.

Miami International Airport. The Miami International Airport is truly the gateway to the Americas. The airport is situated on 3,000 acres of land in the near northwest part of the city. It was the third airport established in the United States and was built in 1912 by a company headed by pioneer aviator Glenn G. Curtiss. From this airfield on June 1, 1937, Amelia Earhart, with Captain Frederick Noonan as copilot, took off on a proposed 27,000-mile flight around the world, the first attempt ever made to encircle the globe at the middle latitudes. The last radio message, July 2, stated the plane was over the Pacific, position doubtful, with half an hour's fuel supply. Plane and pilots were given up for lost on July 18. In 1953, a total of 2,141,854 passengers passed through the airport terminals. Of these, over 600,000 were foreign travelers, making Miami the leading airport of entry of the nation.

Arch Creek Bridge. This natural limestone arch was the original "Gateway to Miami" and a bridge on the Military Trail of the 1800s. Arch Creek Park protects a sliver of tropical hammock that is a known archaeological site, a village of the Tequesta Indians between 500 B.C. and 1300 A.D. Nature trails wind through the lush landscape, scant steps from the busy Biscayne Boulevard. The arch itself collapsed in the 1980s, but has been put back in place with a little human help. A small museum on-site explains the historical and archaeological significance of this small but important park.

Musa Isle Indian Village. Located on the Miami River, the Musa Isle Indian Village was one of the most popular Seminole Indian attractions in the Miami area. The five-acre village opened in 1922 and featured alligator wrestling, reptile and bird exhibits, and Seminole Indians as they lived in their camps.

Metromover. This elevated, electric, free, driverless monorail is a mass transit system that moves people around Downtown Miami. The Metromover tends to attract an odd crowd, including business people, tourists, and vagrants. This Metromover also connects with the Metrorail System that serves a larger Miami area. This transportation system also connects with the Tri-Rail System, which connects Miami with northern destinations as far north as West Palm Beach.

Miami Beach and South Beach

Miami Beach is nearly four miles across Biscayne Bay from Miami, forming the eastern boundary of the bay for about ten miles. It is nearly a mile wide from the bay to the Atlantic Ocean. Until 1914 it was a jungle, one of the neglected islands that reached along the Florida East coast southwesterly toward Key West. It was first connected with Miami by a long, narrow, wooden bridge. A town with broad avenues planted with palm and pine trees was laid out, which eventually became one of the finest resorts in the world. The founders of Miami Beach were of large vision, men who dreamed and planned and achieved in terms of millions.

By the late 1920s there were two causeways connecting Miami and Miami Beach. The glorious skies of this tropical land, the tempered breezes from the Gulf Stream, and the marvels of morning and evening skies, were the gift of nature to every visitor to this beautiful city. Miami Beach, together with the wonder city of Miami, became what has been called "The Nation's Winter Playground."

South Beach is Miami Beach's answer to Cannes where people play at being a star or look for one sauntering down Ocean Drive. An international beat permeates South Beach (called SoBe), and everyone from European glitterati to senior citizens and drag queens dance to it. In the Art Deco District, Technicolor architecture straight out of the 1930s goes hand-in-hand with the next in high fashion and furbelows. SoBe has streetside cafes, white sandy beaches, tropical palms, and lively nightlife. The Art Deco hotels and other structures in SoBe are Miami Beach treasures.

The Aquarium. Located in Miami Beach on Biscayne Bay next to the County Causeway (now MacArthur Causeway), the Aquarium was famous for its exhibition of fish and fish research. Jim Allison built it at a cost of $150,000. In 1926, the Aquarium was razed and Carl G. Fisher built the Floridian Hotel on the site.

Indian Creek. This beautiful waterway runs almost the entire length of Miami Beach, starting at Lake Pancoast at 23rd Street and Collins Avenue, and running straight north through Surfside, Bal Harbour, Golden Beach, Hallandale, and Hollywood, and on into the inland waterway that goes through Fort Lauderdale to the north. This famed waterway is sometimes known as the yachtsman's highway.

Polo in Miami Beach. The first polo field in Florida was located on the south side of Lincoln Road, stretching from Meridian to Lenox and Lincoln Road to 15th Street. The introduction to polo in Miami Beach in 1919 was Carl G. Fisher's ingenious idea. This view of the Nautilus Hotel was taken from the polo field. The Nautilus, built by Fisher, was a six-story luxury hotel with Spanish decorative elements.

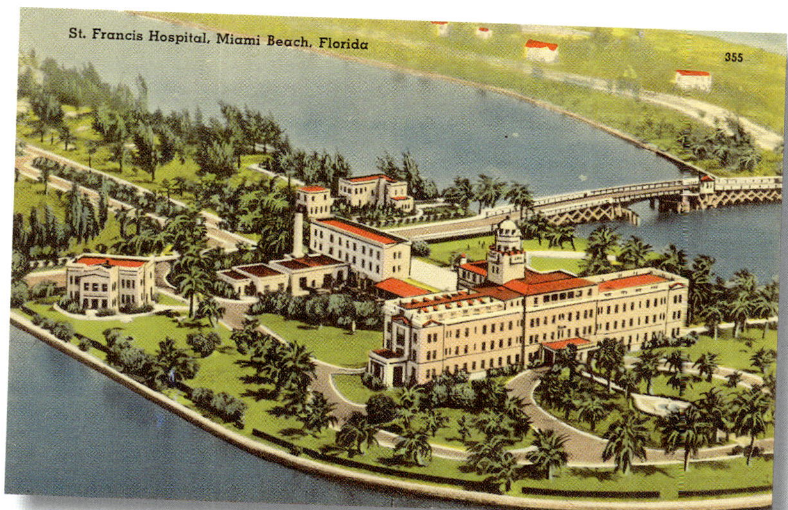

St. Francis Hospital. In 1926, Jim Allison built a hospital at the top of Indian Creek, which he named for himself (Allison Hospital). The Sisters of St. Francis took over the operation of the hospital as the St. Francis Hospital. The St. Francis Hospital is a large, plain stucco building with buff trim and an illuminated cross on a tower, situated on the six-acre grounds on Allison Island in the center of Indian Creek. Constructed in 1925, it cost more than $1 million. In addition to the hospital, there was the Villa Francisco rest home, a swimming pool, tennis courts, laundry, a private dock, and nurses' home.

Joe's Stone Crab Restaurant. Joe Weiss started cooking at Smith's Casino on Miami Beach in 1913. Five years later, following a disagreement with the casino owners, he opened a seafood restaurant on the farthest south street of Miami Beach. Joe's Restaurant, at 227 Biscayne Street, eventually became Joe's Stone Crabs. Hungry diners allow bibs to be tied around their necks and subsequently feast on succulent Florida stone crabs dipped in mustard sauce and served with homemade fries. Many people insist Joe's serves the best key lime pie in the United States. Famous customers include Al Capone, the Duke and Duchess of Windsor, J. Edgar Hoover, Joe Kennedy, and Gloria Swanson. Today, the popular restaurant still serves stone crabs to hungry locals and visitors.

Venice of the South. Both gondolas and gondoliers were imported to ride the Miami Beach waterways on romantic tours for visitors. Carl G. Fisher gave a continental touch to the beach waterways by adding a fleet of Venetian gondolas to his hotel facilities.

Winter Bathing. As this 1920s view of bathers at Miami Beach shows, bathing suits were designed to cover more than they revealed. Beach attire has changed over the years, but the popularity of Miami Beach has not. Warm breezes and the gentle waters of the Atlantic Ocean attract visitors from around the world.

Beautiful Girls on Miami Beach. Many a masculine head turned when these pretty bathers ran down the beach. In order to generate interest in Miami Beach, postcard publishers produced many cards of beautiful girls in bathing suits.

Fun Destination to War Camp. In 1941, the U.S. Army invaded the tourist-oriented city of Miami Beach and turned the fancy hotels into barracks; restaurants and clubs into mess halls; churches and synagogues into classrooms; and streets, beaches and golf courses into drill practice areas. Before World War II ended, one-fourth of the Army Air Force officers and one-fifth of the enlisted men trained at Miami Beach. The Shelborne Hotel is shown in the far right corner.

Carib Theatre. On Lincoln Road in the mid-1950s there was a movie theater on every other block. Miami Beach was a popular choice for movie premiers. Jimmy Stewart and his wife, Gloria, were there in 1954 for the world premier of *The Glenn Miller Story* at the Carib Theatre. The beautiful Carib Theatre, located at 230 Lincoln Road, had a goldfish pond and macaws in the lobby. Before he became a famous broadcaster, Larry King was once an usher at the Carib Theatre. He wore a bow tie, collected tickets, and used a flashlight to help people find their seats in the dark. Other theaters on Lincoln Road were the Lincoln and Colony theatres. Across the street from the Carib Theatre is the Albion Hotel.

Coral Gables

Coral Gables lies southwest of Miami, three miles from the center of the city. The most significant thing about this city is the realization of George E. Merrick's vision of the perfect city, the putting into material concrete forms his artist dream. Merrick's staff included artists, landscape architects, and utility engineers. Denman Fink, an artist of international renown, supervised the artistic growth of Coral Gables, and designed the entrances and Spanish plazas throughout. Coral Gables streets are virtually boulevards. They vary from 50 to 250 feet in width and are broad vistas of beauty, bordered by sidewalks and lighted night by forty-five miles of streetlights. A published summary of things to do in Coral Gables lists no less than twenty-four varieties: tennis, golf, swimming, fishing, horseback riding, athletic contests, baseball, bowling, hiking, rowing, horseshoe pitching, concerts, motoring, sailing, canoeing, pageants, festivals, children's sports, dancing, moving pictures, bridge teas, nature study, entertainments, and tea dances. A series of canals and yacht basins were dredged to connect with Biscayne Bay and afforded winter anchorage for winter visitors and residents of the city. Coral Gables began as an artist's dream and, over the years, became a beautiful city.

Golfers at Play at Granada Golf Course. The nine-hole, 58-acre Granada Golf Course, located adjacent to the Coral Gables Country Club, opened in 1923. It was designed by Langford and Moreau, a leading Chicago golf course architectural firm.

Coral Gables City Hall. The City Hall is surrounded by palms and flower gardens. With its outstanding architecture, it was one of the most beautiful city halls in the country.

The Inn. The Inn at Coral Gables, built in 1922 by the Coral Gables Corporation, was the first hotel in the city. The Inn, located at 303 Minorca Avenue, housed and entertained prospective land buyers who began to arrive in response to George Merrick's phenomenal advertising campaign. It later served as the Coral Gables Lodge and Hotel, the Musician's Club, and, in 1972, was demolished to be used as a parking lot.

Coral Gables Woman's Club and Public Library. The Woman's Club, located at 1001 E. Ponce de Leon Boulevard, was built by the Works Progress Administration (WPA) in 1937 on city-owned land. The structure, which also housed the city library, was built of native coral limestone, and consisted of two one-story buildings with red tile roofs set at right angles and connected by an arcaded patio. The Woman's Club, which was also the Community House, had an auditorium that seated five hundred people.

Merrick Building, University of Miami. The Merrick Building, named for George Merrick's father Solomon, was begun in 1926 on land Merrick had originally given for a permanent campus. The skeleton of the structure stood uncompleted until 1949. Due to a construction time delay, the original Mediterranean design by architect Phineas Paist was abandoned. By 1956, there were almost 13,000 pupils enrolled at the University. It had emerged as a busy, forward-surging educational center. Today the University of Miami is considered one of the Nation's major universities.

Venetian Pool. The prettiest public swimming pool in America is this incredible grotto. A spring-fed wonderland of coral rock caves, cascading waterfalls, a palm-fringed island, and Venetian-style moorings.

Tahiti Beach. Tahiti Beach was one of America's most tropical beaches with swaying coconut palms, thatched roof shelters and inviting waters. It was planned to depict a South Seas setting in the United States. In scenery and atmosphere it is a unique part of the greater Miami area. This six-mile stretch of bayfront was part of a 6,000-acre tract purchased by George Merrick in 1925. Located on Biscayne Bay just south of the Coral Gables Waterway, Tahiti Beach was originally intended to provide guests at the Biltmore Hotel with a salt-water beach. When it opened in 1926, twenty-five authentic Italian gondolas and their gondoliers transported guests from the hotel to the beach via the Coral Gables Waterway. Tahiti Beach was later opened to the general public. In the 1920s and the 1930s it was a haven for nudists and natural healing cults. In the early 1970s the land was used as the site of an exclusive Coral Gables residential subdivision.

Matheson Hammock Park and Beach. Three miles south of Miami (9610 Old Cutler Road) is Matheson Hammock and its beautiful white sand beach on Biscayne Bay, a mecca for tourists and inhabitants of the Greater Miami area. The hammock in this park is a wonderful stand of subtropical jungle. Delightful trails wind beneath huge live oaks, air plants, mangrove trees, palms and native orchids. William Matheson donated the park to the people of Dade County in 1930; the original eighty-four acres was later expanded to six hundred acres. Today, Matheson Hammock Park is the city's oldest and one of the most scenic parks there is.

Key Biscayne

Key Biscayne is known as the site of the Cape Florida Lighthouse and as a protective barrier between the Atlantic Ocean and Biscayne Bay. The lighthouse here was completed in 1825 and remains one of the oldest structures in South Florida. A temporary Army post, Fort Bankhead, was established here during the Second Seminole War (1835-1842). For residents of metropolitan Miami, Key Biscayne became accessible by motor vehicle during the 1940s with the building of the Rickenbacker Causeway and development of an outstanding recreation area, Crandon Park. The causeway took its name from the World War I flying ace, Edward "Eddie" Rickenbacker, and the park from Dade County Commissioner Charles H. Crandon, who was the park plug in public acquisition and development of the oceanside.

The Miami Sequarium, which opened September 24, 1955, is the longest operating oceanarium in America, attracting 600,000 visitors a year. The Bill Baggs Cape Florida State Recreation Area, a 406-acre spread of woods and beach, is located at the southern end of Key Biscayne.

In its short history, the village of Key Biscayne has been a coconut plantation, a launch point for fleeing slaves and the island getaway of Richard Nixon while he was President. Many of the residents own a boat, a windsail, and live in multimillion-dollar villas and high-rises with wraparound views. There are more animal crossing signs than traffic lights in the village.

Cape Florida Lighthouse. The Cape Florida Lighthouse, located on the southeast corner of Key Biscayne, was built in 1825. It was partially destroyed by fire during a Seminole Indian attack in 1836. The lighthouse was rebuilt in 1855 to its present height of 95 feet. It was abandoned in 1878 when the Fowey Rock Light was built further out to sea and nearer the ship lanes. It is still preserved as a landmark. The Cape Florida Lighthouse is just a short distance from downtown Miami.

Hialeah

While Little Havana may be the ideological center of Miami's Cuban-American community, Hialeah is its population center. Bordered by the Miami Canal to the south and LeJeune Road to its east, it's the largest of the outlying Miami communities.

A settlement was established here in 1910 by James H. Bright, a Missouri ranchman, who transformed 1,000 acres of a 14,000 acre track into a grazing meadow for his herd of cows, with a year-round dairy industry in view. In 1917, Glenn H. Curtiss, daredevil aviation pioneer, collaborated with Bright into building a town on the banks of the Miami Canal. The cattle were moved further north. The town was incorporated in 1922; however, the name became associated with the nation's loveliest horse racing track, Hialeah Park. Later a large number of light industry, manufacturers, and warehouses relocated in Hialeah.

A large and important part of the Hialeah community was the Hialeah Park horseracing track, laid out in 1925. Covering 230 acres, it was conceived as a resort facility and modeled after European racing sites such as Longchamps in France. For many years the races, the Mediterranean revival clubhouse, the pink-and-turquoise associated buildings, and the lush formal landscaped gardens, complete with lake, islands, and flocks of pink flamingoes attracted people from all over the world. The park became so famous for the birds that it was designated an official flamingo sanctuary. Horse racing stopped at Hialeah Park in 2001.

Opa-Locka

Glenn H. Curtiss, pioneer of the aviation industry, and ranchman James H. Bright started the community of Opa-Locka during the 1920s Florida land boom. Curtiss is credited with having selected the name Opa-Locka, because the original buildings were reminiscent of a city from the Arabian Nights. Curtiss called it the "Bagdad of Dade County." Curtiss commissioned architect Bernhardt Emil Muller to build the town around the theme of the tales of "The Thousand and One Nights."

Opa-Locka played a big role in shaping our nation's baseball history. Twelve years after Amelia Earhart departed from the Miami Municipal Airport, and sixteen years after the Graf Zeppelin, the second largest airship in history, made use of the local air station as a regular stop on its international flight route, the city of Opa-Locka played host to the "Girls of Summer" professional baseball team. From 1943 to 1954 talented women of the All-American Girls Professional League (AAGPBL), the first and only professional female baseball league in U.S. history, conducted spring training at an Opa-Locka baseball field. The practice field where the glamorous baseball players trained was torn down, replaced by Miami's urban sprawl. Today, the Baseball Hall of Fame in Cooperstown, honors these pioneering women of baseball, and Hollywood has recounted their story in the film "A League of Their Own."

Opa-Locka is located northeast of Hialeah and northwest of downtown Miami. The twenty-first century Opa-Locka is an economically deprived and rundown neighborhood; however, the city still contains much of the Arab architecture for which it was initially famed. The name incidentally is a short form of a Seminole Indian word "opatishawaukalocka," which means "hammock in the big swamp," and is made up of opilwa, meaning swamp, and lako, meaning big.

Hialeah Park. In 1924, the Miami Jockey Club was built on the soggy edge of the Everglades. The Miami Jockey Club later became the Hialeah Race Track. Hialeah Park's 220 acres the embodiment of tropical splendor, was said to have 1,250 royal palm trees, 9,400 Washington palms, and 100,000 shrubs and small plants. Some of the royal palms, eighty feet tall and 150 years old, were brought from the Everglades and Cuba. The vine-covered grandstand and the clubhouse were built in 1931. The wide oval track rings a 92-acre area in lawns and flower beds, surrounding a 32-acre artificial lake in which hundreds of pink flamingos, seen from the grandstand, resemble a bed of pink water lilies. These birds, captured in southern Cuba in 1934, are kept in the park by clipping their wings. This famous racetrack includes stables for over a thousand horses and is one of the most beautiful thoroughbred-racing arenas in America. Hialeah Park is on the National Registry of Historic Places, and has been designated a bird sanctuary by the National Audubon Society. It has been closed since 2001.

Opa-Locka City Hall. Glenn W. Curtiss, aviation pioneer, and James H. Bright developed Opa-Locka during the 1920s. Curtiss selected the name Opa-Locka, because the original buildings were reminiscent of a city from the Arabian nights. Show is the Opa-Locka Moorish fantasy municipal building.

North Miami and North Miami Beach

Located in the northeast area of Greater Miami, North Miami Beach is home to Greynolds Park. Established in 1936, it is one of Greater Miami's oldest parks. The Ancient Spanish Monastery, an actual tenth century monastery brought over from Spain in 1925 by newspaper publisher William Randolph Hearst, was eventually reconstructed in this area in 1952. The Arch Creek Park, a county park in North Miami, is home to a natural stone formation that was used as a roadway bridge for years.

Fisher Island

Fisher Island, accessible only by boat or plane, is a luxurious resort and residential island.

Bal Harbour, Sunny Isles Beach, and Surfside

These three seaside communities north of Miami Beach are only a stone-crab's throw from South Beach. Bal Harbour is an elegant little village with shopping and dining that rivals Fifth Avenue, Rodeo Drive, or the Champs Elysees. Nostalgia buffs like the hotels of Sunny Isles Beach, many designed with whimsical 1950s-style theme motifs. The popular Newport Fishing Pier is located here. The nearby village of Surfside is a quiet residential area with a secluded stretch of shoreline that caters to families.

Coconut Grove

Coconut Grove sits on the shores of Biscayne Bay south of downtown Miami, bordered by U.S. Highway 1, the Rickenbacker Causeway, and the Coral Gables Waterway. The area was originally settled by Bahamian seafarers and a scattering of pioneer families. One of the early residents was Horace Porter. He was only around for a year but in that time he established a post office, which he named Cocoanut Grove. Porter moved on and the post office closed. In 1863, John Thomas Peacock homesteaded 160 acres by the side of Biscayne Bay. The area was filled with a grove of coconut trees. In 1882, Charles Peacock, brother of John, his wife, Isabella and their three sons opened the Bay View House, later called the Peacock Inn, the first hotel in the area. Commodore Ralph Munroe reopened the post office and repainted the sign, dropping the letter "a" from its name.

By 1888 Coconut Grove became a small community of sea enthusiasts, writers, and intellectuals. Many migrant families from the Bahamas Islands also arrived to work at the Peacock Inn, and so Miami's earliest African-American settlement was founded.

In 1919, the city of Coconut Grove was incorporated. Coconut Grove was swallowed up by neighboring Miami in 1925, but over the years independent-minded locals protested the annexation in periodic unsuccessful secession movements More recent attempts at secession have been hamstrung by the fact that Miami City Hall is located in Coconut Grove.

There is a historical marker that describes the impact of the "Bay of Pigs" on Miami at S.W. 27th Avenue and Bayshore Drive in Coconut Grove. The marker reads as follows. In the early months of 1961 Cuban refugees in Miami flew from Opa-Locka airport to Guatemala to become part of the almost 1,300 men of Brigade 2506. The Brigade's Bay of Pigs Invasion on April 17, 1961, resulted in defeat, with over one hundred men killed and the rest imprisoned. The invasion's failure did not destroy the dream of returning to Cuba, but it did make many look at Miami as more than temporary refuge. Careers, education and the starting of new lives became important concerns of the refugees. At the same time the Cuban community anxiously waited while negotiations between the U.S. and Cuba secured the release of the prisoners. Two days before Christmas in 1962 the prisoners began arriving by air at Homestead Air Force Base and were reunited with their families at Dinner Key Auditorium.

Little Havana

In an old section of the city, west of downtown Miami and north of Coral Gables, lies Little Havana, home to several hundred thousand Cuban Americans and other Hispanics. In all, more than half a million Cubans live in the Greater Miami area. Little Havana is the heart and soul of the Cuban immigrant community in the U.S. A trip through this enclave is like traveling to a foreign country. Store signs are in Spanish as is the conversation. Salsa or Rumba music filters through the air, the "guayabera" street vendors in richly embroidered shirts sell fruit and other wares; a plethora of cafes, bars, restaurants and pastry shops offer Cuban and other Latin specialties, including arroz con pollo (chicken and saffron rice), ceviche (raw fish marinated in lemon sauce), fried plantains (a type of Latin American banana), ropa vieja (sliced beef in a tomato sauce), churros (a Cuban pastry) with Cuban café con leche (coffee with milk), or palamilla steaks, served with black beans and white rice. One can also hear the sound of dominoes hitting the tables in Domino Park. Blink and one might think they were in Caracas or Havana. The main street in Little Havana is Calle Ocho (Southwest 8th Street). This street is also the street of parades, protest marches and the famous Calle Ocho Open House, which takes place in March each year.

Little Haiti

The neighborhood of Little Haiti lies within the boundaries of 79th Street to the north, 46th Street to the south, Biscayne Boulevard to the east, and Interstate Highway 95 to the West. Once known as Lemon City, Little Haiti is so named due to the influx of Haitian immigrants. It is a vibrant community, with an interesting blend of Caribbean Culture and American spirit.

Liberty City

Just west of Little Haiti is Liberty City, another active African-American community where civic pride is an art form — literally! Local artists create beautiful murals on the walls of various buildings in the area depicting heroes, both local and world-renowned, of the African-American community.

Overtown

This city is the thriving center of Greater Miami's African-American community. Historical structures located in Overtown are the Lyric Theater, Greater Bethel AME Church, and the house of D. A. Dorsey, Miami's first African-American millionaire. The Miami Arena, home of the Miami Heat basketball team and the NHL's Florida Panthers is located here.

South Miami

South Miami, a community of beautiful homes and a charming commercial district, is located southwest of Coral Gables and downtown Miami. Until the land boom of the 1920s, the area was called Larkins after a pioneering family.

Biscayne/Miami Shores

In the early 1870s, William H. Gleason and William H. Hunt moved up the bay from Miami and founded the community of Biscayne. They brought with them the Miami Post Office, renaming it the Biscayne Post Office. Since the Dade County Court was wherever Gleason was, Biscayne was often the county seat and the meeting place of the county commission. Ephraim T. Sturtevant, Andrew Price, Edward Barnott, and Dr. Richard B. Potter were other settlers of Biscayne. One early visitor was Tuttle, the daughter of Sturtevant and the "Mother of Miami." By the 1880s, many of the early residents were gone and the post office was closed in 1888. Activity was renewed in Biscayne in 1892 with the building of the first county road, from Lantana to Lemon City, through Biscayne, and the post office was reopened. Later a railroad depot and a school were built. In the 1920s, Miami Shores was developed where the community of Biscayne once stood.

Part II:
Miami Past and Present

Chapter Three:
City Overview

Like so many cities in Florida, Miami first came into being as an extension of the military in the Seminole Indian War of the 1830s. In 1835 a fort was constructed on the north bank of the Miami River not far upstream from Biscayne Bay. The fort was named Fort Dallas and is still standing today, a few blocks from the original location. It was moved to Lummus Park, a city recreational park on NW 2nd Street and 3rd Avenue. In 1836 Dade County was named for Major Francis Dade, a soldier who was killed by the Seminole Indians in northwest Florida.

After the Seminole Indian Wars, settlers began to come into the area looking for good farming land to homestead. The federal government was encouraging new settlers by offering homesteads and land at low cost. A small village was established around Fort Dallas by William H. English, who called it Miami. William Brickell, a newcomer from Cleveland, Ohio, arrived in 1870. He opened the first commercial store in the area. His mercantile venture was both a store and a trading post. His customers included both settlers and Seminole Indians. Brickell later added an inn, which was the most popular stopping-over place between Jacksonville and Key West. Roads were poor and hard to maintain. Since most of the travel was over water, the location of his store on Brickell Point, as it was called, at the mouth of the Miami River on the South side, was the main point of interest in Miami (this was previously the location of the most famous Miami-Dade County archaeological site ever, the Miami Circle. Discovery of the 38-foot-diameter circle in September 1998 generated worldwide publicity and led to a successful drive to put the 2.2 acres site in public ownership). Brickell also built his home on what is now known as Brickell Point.

Julia D. Tuttle arrived in Miami in 1880 and purchased 1,200 acres of land on the north side of the Miami River and west from Biscayne Bay. The land cost $12.40 per acre. Land was cheap and Miami had almost no overland transportation. So Julia Tuttle contacted a retired ex-Standard Oil Company executive, Henry Morrison Flagler, who owned the Florida East Coast Railway and a string of resort hotels that stretched from St. Augustine to Palm Beach. The hotels were meant to keep his railroad busy, hauling the rich and famous from the cold northern cities to his string of fancy resort hotels along the east coast of Florida.

By 1890, a small settlement had mushroomed around Fort Dallas. Tuttle promised to hand over half of her extensive acreage if Flagler would extend his railroad to Miami. His first answer was a refusal. Then came the "Big Freeze" of 1894-1895 when the ice was reported to be an inch thick in some parts of northern Florida. She again contacted Flagler sending him orange blossoms and flowers to prove that Miami was below the freezing line. This time, Flagler visited Miami and agreed to bring his Florida East Coast Railway this far south. William Brickell also put in his share of the property, thus Flagler's property included half of the original town site, 640 acres of the best downtown section of Miami of today. Julia also gave Flagler all the land from what is now Flagler Street to the Miami River, except the Dallas Park site. On this property Flagler built the fabulous Royal Palm Hotel and, for many years, it was the winter home for the famous and near famous. The DuPont Plaza Hotel was later built on this site. Work immediately started on bringing the railroad to Miami.

The Florida East Coast Railway reached Miami on April 15, 1896. Three months later, Miami received its charter, and the 480 residents selected John B. Reilly, the first Mayor of Miami, and the tropical town was on its way. The name Miami was derived from the Indian word "Mayaimi," which means "big water." "Mayaimi" was also the Calusa Indian name for Lake Okeechobee.

There is a historical marker about Fort Brickell on Brickell Avenue in Miami. The marker reads as follows. On February 15, 1898, the U.S. battleship *Maine* was blown up in the Havana Harbor and, on April 25, war with Spain was declared. Many Miamians feared a Spanish invasion, in spite of the shallow channel. In response, the U.S. government erected a temporary fortification on Brickell property, one and a half miles south of Brickell Point and five hundred feet east of this marker. The "fort," which commanded the channel, consisted of an earth mound covering the magazine, two guns, and a hundred foot semicircular parapet. The Spanish-American War ended August 12, 1898, and by September the guns had been removed from "Fort Brickell."

Arrival of the railroad brought many of Miami's pioneers; among Flagler's "Men of Action" were Joseph A. McDonald, John Sewell and Everest

G. Sewell. McDonald later became president of the Miami Chamber of Commerce, the Sewell brothers, from Georgia, worked hundreds of African-Americans in clearing land so that buildings could be erected. The Sewells later went into the mercantile business and soon became active in public life. John was mayor four times and Everest was the first president of the Miami Chamber of Commerce and held this position for eight years; later he was elected mayor and held this office many times.

Pioneering in Miami was just that. Harassed by millions of mosquitoes, hundreds of poisonous snakes and continual land-clearing difficulties, the far-seeing pioneers nevertheless labored on with the constant knowledge their territory was blessed with a perfect climate. By 1900 the residents numbered 1,681 and the fame of Miami began to spread across the nation. The period between 1910 and 1920 was of little historical importance except that each winter brought new visitors and most of the old ones returned — many of them purchasing property and delving into real estate. The area began to take on the unmistakable signs of a city.

Miami was involved in aviation during World War I, at Dinner Key and Chapman Field. After the war ended in 1918, Miami's reputation as a tropical paradise spread across the nation, and a steady stream of people looking for the fast dollar and paradise poured into South Florida. By 1920 the population had grown to 29,471 and was growing daily.

The early 1920s brought thousands of fortune hunters. The railroad could not handle the demand for everything from food to building supplies. Hundred of ships of every description were anchored in Biscayne Bay. Everything was in short supply. Downtown streets were jammed with real estate offices, skyscrapers shot skyward, shaky wooden buildings were replaced by heavy modern structures, property values soared and money flowed freer than water. Accommodations sold at fabulous prices as visitors poured into the city.

Inflation was rampant. Perishables such as butter and milk were hard to find. Buildings supplies could not keep up with the demand. Millions of dollars were made and lost every day in the changing real estate market. The boom started dying out in 1925, but it took the great hurricane of September 1926 to deliver the final blow; winds attained a peak velocity of 150 mph ripping through the city. It left much damage in Miami and destroyed the hastily built boom buildings.

Miami had a depression three years before the rest of the nation. People departed the city in droves. Vacant houses and commercial buildings were everywhere. Property reverted to the cities and county for non-payment of taxes. City and County were hard put to provide services. In 1930, Miami had 110,637 people. Miami's recovery during the 1930s was a slow and painful process, but the growth was sound. Visitors again began to come south to the tropical city beside Biscayne Bay, and now her sister paradise over on Miami Beach was the big drawing card. New buildings and hotels were giving Miami a metropolitan look, and the name Magic City began a renewal of her past luster. The railroad was again delivering large crowds of visitors to the tropical paradise. Miami's popularity continued to increase each year. In 1940, the population was 172,172.

World War II found Miami a bustling and thriving city. The proximity of the Gulf Stream with its large cargo and tanker vessels plying its surface caused the U.S. Navy to establish a sonar school, the Submarine Chaser Training Center, and Miami's shoreline along Biscayne Bay was a beehive of Navy "blue and white." Famed bay front hotels were converted into Navy barracks and Bayfront Park became their recreation center. Shipyards, dry-docks, airplane plants, and many products for war use were manufactured in Miami, and thousands of men and women used to leisure became defense and war workers.

Opa-Locka was the home of a large Naval Air Training Base and Supply Center for the Seventh Naval District. The University of Miami in Coral Gables had a flying school activity that trained pilots from all over the world. The Air Force had an Officer Training School on Miami Beach that housed personnel in the famous hotels.

A blimp base with giant hangars, located south of Miami, was the home of the cigar-shaped dirigible whose watchful patrol aided many convoys through submarine infested waters of the south Atlantic coast. West of Miami, airports were developed. The Marine Air Depot received and disbursed thousands of tons of supplies, parts, and material of war by means of transport planes of the air transport and ferry commands. The end of World War II sent many boosters home, who promised to return and they did.

After World War II, the Miami area began a tremendous growth period. The census in 1945 gave Miami 192,122 of which 78.3 percent was white, 21.6 African-American, and 7.4 percent foreign-born. About ninety-three percent of the white permanent population migrated from north and central Florida, Georgia, Alabama, Kentucky, North and South Carolina, Tennessee and many northeastern, mid-western, and western states, thus making it a truly cosmopolitan city.

During 1950 it was estimated that four million people visited Miami, some staying a few hours, some a few days, some a few weeks, and some staying through the winter season. Others still decided to make their homes here. The 1950 census gave Miami a population of 249,276, with the growth continuing through the decade. While stationed at the Marine Corp Air Station at Opa-Locka during 1952-1954, the author witnessed much of this growth.

When Fidel Castro became the dictator of Cuba in 1959, hundreds of thousands of exiles found their way to Miami. This has lent a distinct Latin flavor to the area's restaurants and nightclubs. Little Havana lies in the southwest section of the city. The main drag in the Little Havana section of Miami is SW 8th Street, commonly known as Calle Ocho. This road continues arrow-straight out west of the city and all the way across southern Florida, where, as the Tamiami Trail (U.S. Highway 41), it bisects the Everglades, before swinging north up the Gulf Coast. Miami and Little Havana has become host to thousands of families from Central and South America, and the Caribbean Islands.

The census of 1960 gave Miami a population of 291,688, and the 1970 census 334,859.

In the 1970s, Haitian immigrants started sailing to Miami in rickety wooden boats in search of a better life. Their plight, escaping the severe poverty and iron-fisted dictatorship of their Caribbean homeland, was understandable to the Miami community, but since they were not fleeing a Communist country, their entry into the United States was not as warmly welcomed by the authorities as was that of the Cubans.

In 1984, the television series "Miami Vice," starring Don Johnson and Philip Michael Thomas, turned the city into a pastel-perfect rock video of intrigue and glamour. The glossy images of tropical lushness, beautiful women, fast cars, neon lights, and the downtown skyline gave a boost to the cities economy. Tourists from around the world, eager to experience a tame version of the same scenario, came to seek it out, and Miami became one of the most-talked about cities in America.

The 1990s brought Miami's first Cuban-born mayor, a new professional basketball team, and, unfortunately, Hurricane Andrew, which ripped through South Florida and left 150,000 people homeless.

Miami Circle—PAST. In 1998, workers were demolishing an old Miami building on the south side of the Miami River to make way for a new high-rise condominium. To their surprise, they uncovered a 38-foot diameter circular pattern of holes cut into the limestone bedrock. It was one of the greatest discoveries in Florida archaeology. The circle was examined and it was determined that the holes were used to support posts for a large round council house. The circle was estimated to have been built about two thousand years ago by ancient Tequesta Indians, who lived in the Miami area. The site, now owned by the Miami-Dade County, has been covered with gravel to preserve the area until more studies can be made.

Miami Circle—PRESENT. By the Miami-Dade County purchasing the Miami Circle site, local citizens demonstrated the political will to preserve an important vestige of Miami's heritage. They made room among the city's skyscrapers to preserve a monument of the Tequesta Indians who preceded all of those who now claim Miami as their home. They saved a 2,000-year-old legacy that was almost completely erased. Looking down from the southeastern side of the Brickell Avenue Bridge is the site of the Miami Circle. The Historical Museum of Southern Florida plans to open and operate a park where visitors will have access to this site. Plans include having interpretative panels that tell the story of the site as well as a panoramic mural and native plants. This view also shows the mouth of the Miami River as it empties into Biscayne Bay.

Fort Dallas Barracks—PAST. To see this unpretentious structure one would never suspect that it was linked with the creation of Miami! Pioneer William F. English constructed this building in 1849 at the mouth of the Miami River. Originally used as slave quarters, during the Seminole Wars, the building served as an Army barracks at Fort Dallas. In 1891, one of Miami's pioneer residents, Mrs. Julia B. Tuttle, having previously purchased the building and surrounding property, came here to live. It was largely through her vision and influence that Henry M. Flagler, Florida's great East Coast developer, was induced to extend his railroad into what is now Miami. Mrs. Tuttle subsequently became known as the "Mother of Miami." In 1925, the building — the only structure remaining of the original fort at the time — was later relocated to its present site in Lummus Park.

Fort Dallas Barracks—PRESENT. In 1925, the Miami Woman's Club and the Daughters of the American Revolution (DAR) moved this building to its present location in Lummus Park. The city fenced it off in the late 1980s when the homeless began building shacks around the property. Today the park site includes several other structures in addition to the Fort Dallas building.

Bird's-Eye View of Miami—PAST. In the 1940s, Miami was not only a playground for the leisure class and a winter home for the wealthy, but it was an idea year-round place in which to rest, play and work. This view shows Miami's thriving business district.

Bird's-Eye View of Miami—PRESENT. When founded as a city in 1896, Miami was still a small outpost with only 300 inhabitants. Today, the Miami metropolitan area has a population over five million. Greater Miami is made up of many neighborhoods and towns all within Miami-Dade County. The most famous area is Miami Beach, known as the "American Riviera" and where fun-filled South Beach is located with its historic Art Deco District. It is also home to the largest Latin American population outside of Latin America, making Miami a real cultural melting pot.

Miami Skyscrapers—PAST. This 1940s view of Biscayne Boulevard and the Miami News Tower shows off Miami's luminous skyline.

Miami Skyscrapers—PRESENT. Each year Miami's skyscrapers get taller and taller.

Miami's Skyline—PAST. During the early part of the twentieth century, Miami's shoreline at Biscayne Bay was changed dramatically and decisively when the city purchased the Bayfront land from the Royal Palm Hotel to N.E. 6th Street. In the mid-1920s, dredging began for the fill used to create Bayfront Park and Biscayne Boulevard. Miami's first skyscraper was the ten-story McAllister Hotel, built in 1919. By 1925, Miami was at the epicenter of the Florida Land Boom, and the Bayfront was lined with structural steel skeletons of hotels and office buildings. In this distant 1920s view are: McAllister Hotel, Columbus Hotel, Colonial Hotel, Everglades Hotel, and at the far right, the Miami Daily News Tower.

Miami Skyline—PRESENT. Miami's modern skyline rises behind beautiful Biscayne Bay. The hotels have been replaced with high-rise offices and condominiums.

Prinz Valdemar—PAST. The *Prinz Valdemar*, an old Danish barkentine, sank during a January 10, 1926 storm, blocking the Miami harbor when the city was in greatest need of lumber and supplies in ships waiting outside. The hurricane of September 18, 1926 raised and beached the 242-foot barkentine, which was converted into a 100-room hotel; in 1927, it was fitted out as an aquarium. Live exhibits included sea turtles, stone crabs, lobsters, shrimp, sharks, moray eels, stingrays, manatees, alligators, and crocodiles. The Miami Aquarium was set in sand on Biscayne Boulevard at N.E. 6th Street. Admission was 25 cents. At the entrance, girl artists did portrait sketches for tips, and two monkeys were chained to a revolving iron ladder. In 1952, the ship was dismantled and towed away. The area between 6th and 8th streets became the home of the American Airlines Arena.

American Airlines Arena—PRESENT. The beautiful, sleek $213-million American Airlines Arena, designed by Arquitectonica, opened on New Year's Eve 1999 with a concert by Gloria Estefan. Two days later, the Miami Heat basketball team played their first game in the new 20,000-seat facility. The massive arena and the neon captions that run across the structure's curves are interesting to watch at night.

Bayfront Park—PAST. In 1922 the city of Miami acquired the park site at the foot of Flagler Street from the Florida East Coast Railway for $1 million. Later Elser Pier, its site and riparian rights were purchased by the city for $340,000. Dredging created the municipal yacht Basin and at the same time gave the park its outline. It took seven months to pump over a million cubic yards of sand from the bottom. The 42-acre park was landscaped with about 10,000 flowers and shrubs from tropical countries throughout the world. The park was designed by world-famous landscape artist Warren Henry Manning from Massachusetts. Bayfront Park, located along Biscayne Boulevard between S.E. 2nd and N.E. 6th streets, and extending to Biscayne Bay, was the site where an assassin shot at President Franklin Roosevelt in 1933, killing instead Anton Cermak, the mayor of Chicago. In 1960, the Torch of Freedom was erected in the park. Also, in the 1960s, Bayfront Park was a popular spot for Cuban refugees to visit en route to the nearby Freedom Tower where they were processed for immigration.

Bayfront Park—PRESENT. Bayfront Park is Downtown Miami's breathing space. There are two amphitheaters that host popular open-air concerts. There are many landscaped areas, walkways, a fountain, memorials, and statues. At the southern end of the park is a memorial designed by Japanese sculptor Isamu Noguchi and dedicated to the astronauts and crew who lost their lives in the tragic *Challenger* Space Shuttle explosion. The park also has an amphitheater that puts on nighttime laser-light shows throwing beams of bright colors into the Miami sky. Toward the eastern edge of the park stands a statue of Christopher Columbus given to the city of Miami by the Italian government.

Bayfront Park Activities—PAST. In the 1920s, William Jennings Bryan, perennial Democratic presidential hopeful, conducted an outdoor Bible class on Sundays in Biscayne Park. On weekdays Bryan spoke at the Venetian Pool in Coral Gables. Bryan was a brilliant orator and the leading spokesman for the new city of Coral Gables. He was paid $50,000 a year to extol its virtues. In the mid-1920s, Arthur Pryor's band played in the bandshell. The bandshell was destroyed by fire on March 21, 1928, and later rebuilt. In this view of Bryan's Sunday Bible class, part of the Royal Palm Hotel can be seen in the background.

Bayfront Park Activities—PRESENT. Concerts, special shows, and even outdoor yoga classes are held in Miami's beautiful Bayfront Park. The Bayfront Marketplace, Miami's popular downtown shopping, dining, and entertainment complex, is located on the northern border of the park.

Bayfront Park Activities—PAST. In the 1930s, Bayfront Park consisted of acres of rolling green hills and palm tree gardens skirting the bay. The park also had a unique Moorish-Spanish bandshell that was landscaped with plantings of royal and coconut palms. The bandshell had a yellow stucco stage of oriental design with a blue platform, red-bordered brown curtain, and a series of paintings of Cairo street scenes on either side of the proscenium. The stucco structure was surmounted by two towers with onion-shaped domes and open-air green benches that seated several thousand people for concerts. Behind the bandshell near the bay was the Royal Palm Club, a popular — but illegal — gambling club that made about $2 million a night. The club closed in 1941 and the U.S. Navy took over the building during World War II. The structure burned down after the war.

Bayfront Park Activities—PRESENT. Today Bayfront Park has two amphitheaters where a variety of concerts and activities are held. The park also has a small beach area, with palm trees on Biscayne Bay, which is popular with the locals.

Municipal Steamboat Docks—PAST. In 1898, Henry Flagler built a dock to service steamships traveling between Miami and Nassau and Key West. In 1912, the U.S. Government cut a new channel between South Miami Beach and Fisher Island and across Biscayne Bay. Later, the channel was deepened, and piers and warehouses were added to the Port. Ocean steamers of the Clyde-Mallory, Merchants and Miners, Peninsular and Occidental, Clark, Bull, and other steamship lines operated tour businesses from Miami. Steamships brought thousands of visitors to Miami during the winter.

Bicentennial Park—PRESENT. A new port was constructed on dredged land in Biscayne Bay in the 1960s. In 1972, the Miami City commissioners passed a resolution for the development of Bicentennial Park. On July 4, 1976, Miamians gathered on the bayfront to dedicate Bicentennial Park, built on the site of the former Port of Miami.

Lummus Park—PAST. Lummus Park, named in the mid-1920s after Commissioner J. E. Lummus, was Miami's first city park; it opened in 1909. Located on the Miami River between N.W. Second and Third Streets, the park had two lawn bowling greens, seventy-nine benches, chess and checkers, a croquet playing field, a community house, indoor fireplace, horseshoe, and shuffleboard courts. The park was popular with tourists and a meeting place for many of the old-timers who continued a yearly pilgrimage to this land of sunshine. In 1925, the Miami Woman's Club and the Daughters of the American Revolution had the Fort Dallas officer's quarters moved stone by stone to Lummus Park. This 1939 view shows the Miami skyline with Lummus Park in the foreground. The Miami-Dade County Court House is in the center and the Fort Dallas officer's quarters building is in the lower right corner.

Lummus Park—PRESENT. Lummus Park is now surrounded by a black cast iron fence and contains several structures, including the old Fort Dallas officer's quarters (on the right) and a "cracker house" (on the left).

Dinner Key—PAST. In the beautiful Coconut Grove section of Miami, on Biscayne Bay about five miles south of downtown Miami, is Dinner Key. Picnickers in sailboats gave the key its name. In World War I, it was a Naval Air Base. In 1930, Pan American World Airways erected huge hangers and a terminal for its Clipper airships and Sikorsky S-42s at Dinner Key. Arriving planes would be hauled up a ramp on beaching wheels so that passengers could unload. Pan Am inaugurated flying boat service to Latin America from this terminal. The U.S. Government dredged the first channel on history especially for aircraft. Over 100,000 visitors a month came to see the giant Flying Clippers. In World War II, Navy and Pan American operated flying boats here until Latin American airports built for hemispheric defense enabled use of more economical landplanes. The City of Miami purchased Dinner Key in 1946.

Dinner Key—PRESENT. Today Dinner Key is the home of the Miami City Hall, an auditorium, and a beautiful marina that has moorings and facilities for power and sailboats. The City Hall is located in the old Pan American terminal.

Chapter Four:

Changing Streets and Byways

Many of Miami's streets are named for influential residents, including:

Flagler Street — Henry M. Flagler's East Coast Railway made Miami possible. Before 1896, there was no easy way to move people and goods in and out of Miami. The railroad arrived in April 1896, and Miami was incorporated in July.

Brickell Avenue — William and Mary Brickell owned a trading post on the south side of the Miami River in the late 1800s. Everything south of the river was called Brickell for years.

Rickenbacker Causeway — Named after World War pilot Eddie Rickenbacker. He later became the president of Eastern Air Lines, which was based in Miami.

MacArthur Causeway — The Dade County Commission, during World War II, honored the defender of Bataan, General Douglas MacArthur, by renaming the County Causeway linking Miami and Miami Beach across Biscayne Bay.

Julia Tuttle Causeway — Connecting Miami and Miami Beach, this causeway (also Interstate 195) was named after Julie Tuttle, the "Mother of Miami."

Kendall Drive — Named for Henry John Broughton Kendall, a director of the Florida Land and Mortgage Company, which bought the land that is now Kendall from the State of Florida in 1883.

John Kennedy Causeway — Named for President John F. Kennedy, it connects Miami and Miami Beach.

Twelfth Street Looking East—PAST. In this 1920s view of 12th Street are the McCrory's, Seminole, and Halcyon hotels (left side of street) and the Biscayne Hotel (right side of street). Twelfth Street was later renamed Flagler Street.

Flagler Street Looking East—PRESENT. The old hotels are gone and have been replaced with office buildings and commercial shops. Flagler Street was formerly 12th Street.

Flagler Street from Bayfront Park—PAST. Flagler Street was the heart of downtown Miami. The McAllister Hotel is on the right.

Flagler Street from Bayfront Park—PRESENT. The 50 Biscayne Building replaced the old McAllister Hotel on the right. The One Biscayne Tower is on the left. The Alfred I. DuPont Building is behind the 50 Biscayne Building.

Flagler Street in Downtown Miami—PAST. Nowhere in Miami was there more action than on Flagler Street in 1925. "Skyscrapers" began to reach for the clouds, and Florida's premier city was being built on the tropical banks of Biscayne Bay and the Miami River. Henry Flagler's 28-year old Royal Palm Hotel was the centerpiece for the growing city. Only three blocks away, construction was going on virtually day and night on buildings bearing the names "Seybold," "Congress," "Olympia," and "Ingraham." In this view looking east toward the Biscayne Bay, on the north side (left) of Flagler Street, are the Seminole Hotel (foreground), First National Bank Building (tall building in the center), and, in the distance, the Halcyon and McAllister hotels.

Businesses on Flagler Street—PAST. Throughout the early twentieth century, a wide range of businesses located on Flagler Street, including: hotels — Biscayne, Halcyon, McCrory's, and Seminole; banks — Bank of Biscayne, First National Bank, and Florida National Bank and Trust; theaters — the Olympia and State; retail stores — Burdines, Kress, Woolworth, and Walgreen Drugs; office buildings — Alfred I. DuPont, Seybold, Biscayne; and the Dade County (now Miami-Dade County) Court House.

Flagler Street in Downtown Miami—PRESENT. The easternmost corner of the old Seminole Hotel structure can be seen in this view. The First National Bank Building still stands (red-brick building in the center), the Alfred I. DuPont Building replaced Halcyon Hotel, and the 50 Biscayne Building replaced McAllister Hotel. On the far right is the One Biscayne Tower at the southwest corner of Flagler Street and Biscayne Boulevard.

Businesses on Flagler Street—PRESENT. Today Flagler Street is still Miami's major downtown roadway, although of a quite different sort from the Roaring Twenties. The six blocks between Biscayne Boulevard on the east and the Metro-Dade Cultural Center on the west throb with the activities of Cuban Americans and other Hispanics. Strolling the street is like taking a trip to Latin America. Yet the Miami of the 1920s still breaks through, particularly in the form of the still-imposing Miami-Dade County Court House, at Flagler Street and N.W. 1st Avenue; the thirteen-story Biscayne Building at 19 W. Flagler Street; and the ten-story former Olympia Vaudeville Theater at 174 E. Flagler Street.

Looking East on Flagler Street—PAST. Flagler Street was the main east and west thoroughfare of downtown Miami. A streetcar is surrounded by automobiles in this 1930s view. Burdines Department Store and Kress 5 & 10 Store are on the right side of this street view. On the left side are the McCrory's and Seminole hotels, State Theater, First National Bank, the Alfred I. DuPont building, and, in the distance, McAllister Hotel.

Looking East on Flagler Street—PRESENT. In this view is the Sun Trust Building and, behind it, One Biscayne Tower.

Downtown Miami's Main Shopping District—PAST. In this Flagler Street view, on the right side, are State Theater, the Seminole Hotel with its colorful balcony, McCrory's Hotel, and the Bank of Biscayne Building. Behind the Biscayne Building is the tip of the Miami-Dade County Court House. On the left are Woolworth's and Burdine's.

Downtown Miami's Main Shopping District—PRESENT. The balconies are gone, but the old Seminole and McCrory's hotel structures and the Biscayne Building are still standing. The peak of the Miami-Dade County Court House is still visible behind the Biscayne Building.

Looking West on Flagler Street—PAST. In the early 1900s, Flagler Street was the shopping, theatrical, civic, and industrial heart of this tropical sunshine city. On the right are the First National Bank, State Theater, the Seminole and McCrory hotels, and the Biscayne Building.

Looking West on Flagler Street—PRESENT. On the right side of Flagler Street are the old First National Bank Building, the old Seminole Hotel structure, and the Biscayne Building. The tip of the Miami-Dade County Court House is behind the Biscayne Building. Today the old First National Bank Building has been transformed into the Flagler First Condominiums.

Biscayne Boulevard—PAST. Biscayne Boulevard presented a picture of extreme beauty — three rows of islands supporting Royal Palms, walkways, and ample parking space, bounded on the east by Bayfront Park and on the west by the modernistic McAllister, Miami Colonial, Columbus, Alcazar, Everglades, and Biscayne Terrace hotels. The Boulevard is part of U.S. Highway 1, which begins at Fort Kent, Maine, at the Canadian border, and ends at Key West, the southernmost city in the United States. This 1950s view shows hotel row (on the left) and, on the right, Bayfront Park, the Miami Public Library, and the Amphitheater.

Biscayne Boulevard—PRESENT. Palm-lined parking islands still separate Bayfront Park from the commercial businesses along the west side of Biscayne Boulevard. However, most of the old hotels were replaced with high-rise commercial buildings.

Biscayne Boulevard—PAST. U.S. Highway 1 and Biscayne Boulevard are one and the same. It is one of the most impressive boulevards in the world. Bounded on the east by picturesque Bayfront Park, and on the west by luxury hotels, it is divided into broad traffic arteries by rows of stately Royal Palms. The first two hotels in this 1940s view are the McAllister and Columbus hotels. The Miami Daily News Tower can be seen in the distance.

Biscayne Boulevard—PRESENT. Biscayne Boulevard is still one of Miami's most beautiful streets. Shown are the 50 Biscayne Building, Bank of America "New World Tower," Continental Building, and the Holiday Inn. These buildings replaced the structures on hotel row. The Freedom Tower (old Miami Daily News Tower) can be seen in the distance. In the foreground is part of the tract for the Metromover, Miami's downtown people mover that opened in 1986.

Sears, Roebuck Store on Biscayne Boulevard—PAST. The 1920 Sears, Roebuck, and Company Building was located at a Biscayne boulevard intersection with a spectacular view of Biscayne Bay. The intersection was originally designed with a traffic-calming circle, or roundabout. Automobile drivers regularly cruised the roundabout, taking in the sights. The Sears, Roebuck, and Company Building, with its majestic white tower overlooking the roundabout, became a beacon to the area. Although the roundabout no longer exists, the tower continues to mark a special place in Miami's history and future. The Sears Building, Miami's second earliest known Art Deco building after the Masonic Lodge, became the Greater Miami Performing Arts Center. In the center of this 1940s view is the Miami Daily News Tower building.

Greater Miami Performing Arts Center—PRESENT. The old Sears Tower still stands as part of the 570,000 square foot Greater Miami Performing Arts Center. The Center, designed by world-renowned architect Cesar Pelli, anchors the Miami Arts, Media, and Entertainment District. In the center of this view is the Freedom Tower (the old Miami Daily News Tower) building.

Brickell Avenue—PAST. A highway, originally built of coral rock through a hammock covered with a dense jungle growth from the Miami River to Coconut Grove, was used by the pioneers between these two settlements long before Miami was incorporated. Originally nothing more than an Indian path, it was later named Coconut Grove Road and later the name was changed to Brickell Avenue in honor of the Brickell family, early pioneers. The road was "rocked" in 1896 and took on its present form of four lanes with a center island in 1911.

Brickell Avenue—PRESENT. Brickell Avenue is Miami's most glamorous commercial street. Around 1916 the avenue became known as "Millionaires' Row" as many prominent industrial people built mansions on the bluff overlooking Biscayne Bay. The road was rezoned for high-rises in the 1950s, resulting in many of the homes being replaced with modern skyscrapers. Brickell Avenue boasts towers of mirrored glass and steel that oversee some of the area's most coveted views of the Atlantic Ocean and Biscayne Bay.

Avenue D Street Scene—PAST. There were no big traffic problems in downtown Miami when this view of Avenue D, the city's first street, was taken in the early 1900s. The streets were sand, and automobiles mixed with buggies. Buildings were solid stone and brick. The Miami Hotel is on the right and almost next door, down the street, is the Majestic Saloon. The Miami Hotel was a large frame structure built by Julia Tuttle, founder of Miami. It was on this street that 368 settlers, on a steamy summer day in July 1896, voted to incorporate Miami as a city. Avenue D later became Miami Avenue.

Miami Avenue Street Scene—PRESENT. At the turn of the twentieth century, Avenue D was the original business district of Miami. After a 1901 fire destroyed their businesses, merchants rebuilt on what is now Flagler Street. Only a handful of commercial businesses relocated on Miami Avenue (formerly Avenue D). In the center of this view is the 1914 Waddell Building, located at 24-36 Miami Avenue. Built by Miami realtor, E. A. Waddell, the building accommodates stores below and apartments above. It is one of the last arcaded storefronts in Downtown Miami that retains its original façade.

Chapter Five:
City, Business, and Religious Structures

Post Office and Custom House—PAST. The Post Office and Custom House, constructed in 1912 on the corner of N.E. 1st Avenue and N.E. 1st Street, was the first federal building in the city. In 1937, the building became the country's first savings and loan.

Post Office and Custom House—PRESENT. In September 2009, Miami's old Post Office and Custom House was unoccupied and "FOR SALE".

Dade County Court House—PAST. The original Dade County Court House, built in 1899, was a two-story wood frame building located on the Miami River, just east of the old Miami Avenue bridge. This structure was replaced in 1904 by the neoclassical-style building shown. An elegant ionic column portico, a classical pediment, rusticated external walls, and an impressive dome on top of an octagonal tower are attributes of this building. The courthouse was not adequate to handle the clerical work associated with the Miami boom years of the mid-1920s. Between 1925 and 1928, a new courthouse was built around the old one, thus allowing business transactions to continue as long as possible.

Miami-Dade County Court House—PRESENT. In 1928, Miami had a new 28-story neoclassical courthouse that, at the time, was the tallest building in the south. This impressive skyscraper, located at 73 West Flagler Street, is easily spotted from just about anywhere in downtown Miami. A slender building with a striking ziggurat root, the courthouse is shaped like a rocket poised for lift-off. The $4-million courthouse structure remained Miami's loftiest building until the 1970s. Inside, beautiful mosaics swirl across the ceiling and ornate brass designs embellish the doors and wall lamps. The imposing Miami-Dade County Court House is topped with a pyramid where vultures tend to roost during the winter months. During past years, the top nine floors served as a prison, from which more than seventy prisoners escaped.

Miami Public Library—PAST. The library, located at the foot of Flagler Street in Bayfront Park, opened to the public July 1951. The library contained 61,000 square feet of floor space, was completely air-conditioned, contained 63,000 volumes, and cost $1,250,000. The building, designed by Stewart and Skinner of Miami, was completely faced with marble. In the early 1980s, the structure was demolished and the library moved to the new Cultural Center on West Flagler Street.

Old Library Site—PRESENT. Today, the site of the Old Miami Public Library is a wide paved walkway from Biscayne Boulevard to Biscayne Bay. The new Miami-Dade Public Library, located at 101 West Flagler Street in the sprawling Metro-Dade Cultural Center, is perhaps the most extensive in the Southeast with some 700,000 volumes.

Looking South from Pan American Drive at Dinner Key—PAST. In 1931, Pan American Airways opened a terminal at Dinner Key and made daily flights to Latin America and the Caribbean. Whenever a Pan Am Clipper was departing or arriving, large crowds gathered to watch. Onlookers would line the observation deck of the terminal. As many as 100,000 visitors a month came to see the giant clipper flying boats. When President Franklin D. Roosevelt flew to Casablanca to meet Winston Churchill and Joseph Stalin in 1943, he left from the Pan American Airways terminal. This flight required 10,964 miles and marked the first time that a president flew while in office. The Pan Am's terminal was sold to the City of Miami in 1946.

Looking South from Pan American Drive at Dinner Key—PRESENT. The City of Miami purchased Pan Am's Dinner Key base in 1946 for use as a waterfront park. The terminal was used as marina offices and the Marina Restaurant until 1954 when it became the Miami City Hall. It remains Miami City Hall today.

Miami News Tower/Freedom Tower—PAST. Built in Spanish baroque style to house the offices of the *Miami Daily News*, this stately tower stands out from the ultramodern skyscrapers with which it shares the Miami skyline. The *Miami Daily News* was the oldest newspaper in South Florida. First published in 1896, it was known as the *Miami Metropolis*. The name was changed to the *Miami Daily News* in 1923. The *News* moved into Miami's first skyscraper, the famous News Tower, in 1925. The tower was built by James M. Cox, *Miami Daily News* owner and former governor of Ohio, for $800,000. The Spanish Renaissance Revival style tower, modeled after the Giralda Tower in Seville, Spain, is 260-feet high with eighteen stories. The structure was designed by the architectural firm of Schultze and Weaver. The formal opening of the tower was observed by the publishing of the largest-ever single issue of a newspaper at that time — 504 pages, 1,200 stories, 1,000 photographs, and twenty-two sections. It took fifty carloads of newsprint to publish the edition, which held the record for forty years until the *New York Times* surpassed it with a 946-pager.

Miami News Tower/Freedom Tower—PRESENT. The structure at 600 Biscayne Boulevard served as home to the *Miami Daily News* for thirty-two years. After the *Miami Daily News* moved in 1957, the building remained vacant until 1962. From this time on until 1974, the U.S. Government used the tower building as a processing center for Cuban refugees. It was symbolically renamed the Freedom Tower, which would make its mark as the Miami equivalent of New York's Ellis Island — the place where nearly 500,000 Cuban refugees began new lives in a country free of political oppression. In 1979, the structure was listed in the National Register of Historic Places. Restored in 1989, the Freedom Tower is one of Miami's finest historical structures.

Alfred I. DuPont Building—PAST. An Art Deco jewel built between 1937 and 1938, the DuPont Building was designed by Marsh and Saxelby of Jacksonville. The seventeen-story structure is 217 feet and eight inches high. Located at 169 East Flagler Street, on the site of the former Halcyon Hotel, the DuPont Building served as the southeastern seat of the Florida National Bank and Trust system. During World War II the U.S. Navy took command of Miami's only post-boom skyscraper, making it their regional headquarters. People promptly nicknamed the DuPont Building the "U.S.S. Neversink."

Alfred I. DuPont Building—PRESENT. This structure is an excellent example of the conservative Depression Modern style of architecture — solid and block-like on the outside, with most of the ornamentation hidden in the interior. Many architectural and design elements, including brass bas-relief elevator doors, lavishly decorated ceilings, and teller screens, have been preserved. Although the address is "Flagler Street," the building architecturally faces Biscayne Bay.

First National Bank—PAST. The First National Bank of Miami was organized June 19, 1902, by Edward C. Romfh, the Anthony brothers, E. M. Brelsford, and W. H. Spitzer. In 1922, this striking new building was erected at the northeast corner of 12th Street (since renamed Flagler Street) and 1st Avenue to house the institution. The bank structure was Miami's tallest and most elegant skyscraper at the time.

Flagler First Condominiums—PRESENT. The First National Bank building became the Southeast First National Bank of Miami in 1974. Cen-Trust Savings and Loan acquired the old First National Bank building in the 1980s and made several modifications to the structure. Rok Enterprises later restored the exterior to its 1920s grandeur and transformed it into the Flagler First Condominiums.

Scottish Rite Masonic Temple—PAST. The Scottish Rite Masonic Temple, located adjacent and north of Lummus Park, was built in 1924. The three-story tall structure, with four Doric columns on the street side, is beautifully embellished and has a ziggurat-shaped mass on the roof, capped by a cupola. The 1,200-seat auditorium has a stage and dressing rooms adequate for operatic productions. The temple also includes a large ballroom and other lodge rooms. Designed by the architectural firm of Kiehnel & Elliott, for many years the temple offered the public theatrical productions in the large auditorium.

Scottish Rite Masonic Temple—PRESENT. The Scottish Rite Temple is a great exercise in Beaux-Arts styling — a striking pyramidal building with an imposing set of steps leading up to it. It was designed three years before the Expositions des Arts Decoratifs in Paris, France, predating the style now called Art Deco. Yet with its flat, geometric, stylized ornament and its foreshortened "skyscraper" shape, the Scottish Rite is clearly a precursor to the "modern" buildings that were to follow.

Gesu Catholic Church—PAST. Miami's first Roman Catholic Church was established in 1896. The Gesu Church was built in 1922 on a site that Henry M. Flagler had donated in 1897. The main part rises to four stories, with a belfry and a large stained-glass rose window above the main entrance, while the interior has sixteen additional stained-glass windows, several large painted murals, and intricately carved marble altar screens and railings. The church is known for its beautiful stained-glass windows and exquisite altar.

Gesu Catholic Church—PRESENT. The Gesu Church is one of downtown Miami's few remaining historical landmarks. It is the oldest church in Miami to remain on its original site. Since 1959, when Cubans first arrived in Miami, Gesu Catholic Church has served the Cuban communities' religious and humanitarian needs. In 1974, the church was listed on the National Register of Historic Places.

Chapter Six:
Waterways

Miami Bayfront—PAST. Biscayne Bay came up to the Boulevard in the 1910s. The area in the foreground, occupied by docks and boats, was to be filled in 1925 for Bayfront Park and Biscayne Boulevard. Stretching across the bay in the distance is the wooden Collins Bridge, replaced later by the Venetian Causeway. Traffic was light when this view was taken. Note the trees that lined the bay's side of the boulevard.

Miami Bayfront—PRESENT. In this view are Biscayne Bay in the foreground, Bayfront Park, and the skyscraper buildings that line the west side of Biscayne Boulevard. The two tall structures on the left are One Biscayne Tower, built in 1973, and 50 Biscayne Building.

Burlingame Island—PAST. In 1916, Margaret Burlingame purchased a five-acre spoil bank she named Burlingame Island. It can be seen to the top left side of the Brickell Trading Post. Over the years the land, which was barely visible to anyone except the Brickells, got bigger with each deepening of the mouth of the Miami River. It had grown to twenty acres by 1943 when Edward Claughton bought it and renamed it Claughton Island.

Brickell Key—PRESENT. In 1970, Hong Kong-based Swine Properties bought Claughton Island, renamed it Brickell Key, and transformed it into a luxury enclave of apartments, restaurants, office buildings, and the Mandarin Oriental Hotel, built in 2000. Downtown Miami is in the background. The island is connected to the mainland by a causeway.

Collins Bridge—PAST. John S. Collins, landowner in both Miami and Miami Beach, constructed the longest wooden bridge in the world (two and one-half miles long) to connect Miami Beach to Miami. On May 23, 1913, Thomas J. Pancoast and his family were the first people to drive across Biscayne Bay from Miami on the newly constructed Collins Bridge. It opened formally a few weeks later, on June 12. This view shows spectators watching the first automobiles setting out from Miami en route to the beach. In 1926, this bridge was replaced by the Venetian Causeway.

Venetian Causeway—PRESENT. The Venetian Causeway (a toll causeway), which opened to the public March 1, 1926, is a beautiful link between downtown Miami and Miami Beach. The roadway crosses several islands and residential neighborhoods. Shown is the western end of the causeway, with the city's towering hotels and condominiums in the background.

Boats in Biscayne Bay—PAST. The City Yacht Basin drew more visitors than any other point of interest in downtown Miami. Operating year-round were yachts that could be chartered for deep-sea fishing with more than 600 varieties of fish to be reeled in. Sightseeing boats also offered many interesting trips: *Seven Seas*, residential island cruise of Miami and Miami Beach; *Uncle Sam*, Venetian Islands, Deering Estate, Florica Keys; *Nikko*, Miami Beach cruise; *Southern Cross*, all-day trip to Fort Lauderdale; *Mermaid*, glass-bottom views of marine life; *Seminole Queen*, Miami River and Indian Village; and *Island Queen*, Miami Beach estates and the Florida Keys. Almost any time of the year the bay is dotted with private yachts, pleasure boats, and picturesque sailboats.

Boats in Biscayne Bay—PRESENT. The protected waters of the Biscayne Bay have long provided excellent opportunities for boating and fishing. Someone once estimated that in Miami one of every seven families owned a boat. The Biscayne Bay area pleasure boat facilities are among the largest and best in the country. In addition to the facilities for boats that stay afloat all the time, landing ramps are provided at many marinas and boating clubs for weekend boatmen and their trailer-rolled small craft. The miles of beaches, Bayfront parks, and causeways also afford launching for small boats.

In 1898, railroad tycoon Henry Flagler built a dock to service steamships traveling between Miami, Nassau, and Key West. The first Port of Miami was later established at this location. A new port was constructed on dredged land in Biscayne Bay in the 1960s. In 1976, the original port area was developed into Bicentennial Park.

Twelfth Street Dock—PAST.

Bicentennial Park—PRESENT.

Port of Miami—PAST. Although the Miami River served the Tequesta Indians and other Native Americans in Florida for thousands of years, the area does not have a good natural harbor. Instead, the Port of Miami was developed in Biscayne Bay after the city was founded in 1896. Henry Flagler, whose Florida East Coast Railway helped to open Florida for development, had a channel dredged from the Miami River to Cape Florida to accommodate steamships from Key West and Nassau. In the wake of Flagler's success, appeals were made to Congress for funding for a deep-water port to enhance trade. Beginning in the early part of the twentieth century the Port of Miami was crated. The first coastal passenger liner to dock in Miami was the SS *Apache*, with two hundred passengers, on November 23, 1924. In the 1920s, passenger service to New York and Baltimore began, followed by links to Havana, Cuba, in the next decade.

Port of Miami—PRESENT. In 1965, the Port of Miami was established on Dodge Island, still in full view of Downtown Miami. The port became the largest cruise ship port and Miami was often called the "Cruise Capital of the World." The Port of Miami handles an estimated seventy-five percent of all cruise ship passengers worldwide. Several million passengers come through the port annually. Nine major cruise lines with around two dozen ships sail out of Miami to exotic destinations throughout the Caribbean, Bahamas, and beyond. In addition to cruise travel, the Port of Miami does a substantial amount of commercial import-export trade.

S.S. Florida Steamship Arriving in Miami—PAST. The Peninsular & Occidental Steamship *S.S. Florida* passes through the channel at Miami upon arrival from Havana, Cuba. The ship sailed from Miami on Mondays, Wednesdays, and Fridays, and from Havana on Tuesdays, Thursdays, and Sundays. The *S.S. Florida* was the symbol of romantic trips to the Caribbean. The land mass in the foreground is the County Causeway (later the MacArthur Causeway).

Carnival Fantasy Cruise Ship Arriving in Miami—PRESENT. After World War II, the cruising industry really began to grow. By the late 1940s and early 1950s, ships were departing Miami on a regular schedule of cruises to Havana, Nassau, and Caribbean ports. By 1976, the Port of Miami had become the cruising capital of the world. In this view, the Carnival Cruise Lines *Fantasy* arrives in Miami from Nassau. The long roadway by the ship is the MacArthur Causeway.

Cruise Ship Leaving Miami—PAST. The southern tip of Miami Beach and the Miami Beach Kennel Club can be seen in the background.

Cruise Ship Leaving Miami—PRESENT. In this view, Miami Beach is on the left, Fisher Island is in the top right, and the eastern end of the MacArthur Causeway is in the bottom right.

Downtown Miami from the Miami River—PAST. Looking across Miami River to Miami's downtown business district, who would have imagined just a century ago that the quiescent Miami River would witness so much history, much less serve as a critical lifeline for one of the most important cities in the hemisphere?

Downtown Miami from the Miami River—PRESENT. Downtown Miami is now a collection of modern high-rise structures.

Brickell's Trading Post on the Miami River—PAST. In the early 1900s, as a city was arising on the north bank of the Miami River, a bustling Indian trade was nearing the end of its third decade of activity on the south bank. There, situated near the mouth, was the thriving Brickell Trading Post, shown in the top right part of this view along with the Brickell home. Miccousukee/Seminole clients poled down river from their Everglades redoubts in dugout canoes, bringing with them egret plumes, coontie starch, alligator skins, and eggs. They exchanged these goods for manufactured items at the trading post. The Royal Palm Hotel, park, and riverfront is on the north (left) side of the Miami River.

Southeast View Along the Miami River—PRESENT. The Sheraton Biscayne Bay Hotel (far right) now occupies the site of the Brickell Trading Post and home. In the center is Brickell Key, with many ultra-modern structures.

Miami River—PAST. One of the shortest rivers in the world, it is only seven miles long. During the pioneer days of Miami, the Seminole Indians traversed this stream to paddle in from the Everglades, their canoes loaded with pelts and skins for the trading post located at the mouth of the river. It was also used as a water supply by pirates and Spanish explorers who once frequented these shores. This postcard, mailed in 1916, shows a tourist boat on a narrow segment of the Miami River, near the head of navigation.

The Miami River—PRESENT. Today both sides of the Miami River are filled with modern hotels, condominiums, office buildings, and other high-rise structures. In the center of this view is the Metrorail bridge, built in 1984.

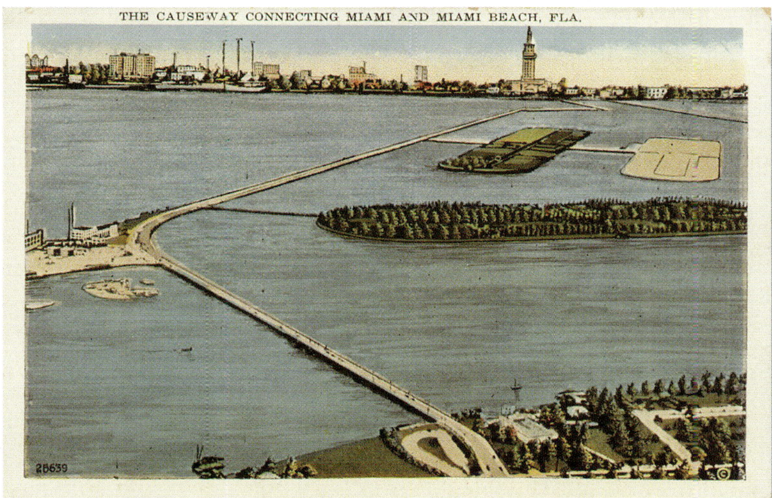

Star Island—PAST. The County Causeway (now MacArthur Causeway) connects Miami and Miami Beach. Shown are Star (center) and Palm islands and the beginning of Hibiscus Island (top right). The islands are reached from the causeway via bridges. These islands were man-made soon after the Miami Beach fills had been completed, surrounded by the iridescent waters of the Biscayne Bay and landscaped with hundreds of tropical trees, palms, and flowers. The Miami News Tower (later Freedom Tower) and downtown Miami can be seen in the background. Miami Beach is at the bottom right.

Star Island—PRESENT. In this view, Star Island is to the left of the MacArthur Causeway (bottom left). The island is now occupied by beautiful residential mansions. Also shown is the southern tip of Miami Beach (top left), Fisher Island (top right), and a cruise ship leaving for ports in the Caribbean.

Flagler Monument—PAST. Carl G. Fisher built this three-acre island, erected the monument to Henry Morrison Flagler, and presented it to the city of Miami Beach. At the base of the central spire are four huge statues representing Prosperity, Industry, Education, and Pioneering, which were all accomplishments of this great Florida empire builder. Miami Beach is in the background.

Flagler Monument—PRESENT. A view of the Flagler Monument from Biscayne Bay. Miami Beach's high-rise buildings can be seen in the background. The monument, which is 100 feet and six inches tall, is lit at night by floodlights. The Flagler Monument is a fitting tribute to a pioneer, a dreamer, and a builder.

Fisher Island—PAST. A prominent black businessman named Dana A. Dorsey bought Fisher Island to start a resort for African Americans who were prohibited from vacationing in Miami. Carl Fisher bought the island from Dorsey in 1919 and later traded it for William K. Vanderbilt's 250-foot yacht and its crew. Vanderbilt built a Spanish-Mediterranean-style mansion on this 216-acre island. Located just off the southern tip of Miami Beach, Fisher Island can only be reached by helicopter, private boat, or ferry.

Fisher Island—PRESENT. Today Fisher Island can be reached by a ferry from a terminal off the MacArthur Causeway. Air-conditioned ferries depart every fifteen minutes around the clock and the trip takes ten minutes. This tiny island is the richest place per capita in the country. Boatloads of sugary white sand from the Bahamas Islands were used to build a beach. Along this mile-long beach are condominium pads that range from $1 million to $7 million. The Fisher Island Hotel & Resort, located at 1 Fisher Island Drive, is pretty well established as the island's exclusive hotel with eight bars or restaurants. The island has a 9-hole golf course and is reported to be the most expensive address in the Miami area.

Chapter Seven:
Hotels

Royal Palm Hotel—PAST. Henry M. Flagler's famous Royal Palm Hotel, finished in 1897, made Miami an important tourist resort. The five-story Royal Palm, surrounded by groves and gardens, looked out on the beautiful blue waters of the Biscayne Bay and the Miami River. The Royal Palm was self-sufficient, offering its guests fishing excursions, golf, sight-seeing, the finest cuisine available, and dancing in the evenings to music played by the hotel orchestra. Guests dressed for dinner. Waiters were imported from Europe. The very life of Miami was tied to the Royal Palm. Flagler's utilities that supplied his hotel with electric power, water, and ice also supplied Miami. The Royal Palm was 680 feet long (more than twice the length of a football field), 267 feet wide, and five stories tall. The hotel had 450 rooms, a grand ballroom, magnificent dining rooms, elevators, ice and laundry plants, and a beautiful park. The hotel, a wooden structure at the mouth of the Miami River, opened in a blaze of electric light. With less than twenty years since Thomas A. Edison invented the incandescent lamp and scarcely more than ten years since the country's first central generating plant was put into service, the electric lighting of the Royal Palm was a milestone in Miami progress. The Royal Palm had Miami's first swimming pool and bathing casino. The swimming pool was filled with salt water from the Biscayne Bay. Locals were allowed to use the pool during the summer off-season. Charge for adults was 25 cents. On August 23, 1926, a hurricane severely damaged the Royal Palm. The hotel closed after the 1928 winter season. The building stood empty until 1937 when the last extant section of the old Royal Palm was demolished.

Downtown Miami—PRESENT. A large part of Downtown Miami now occupies the area once occupied by the Royal Palm Hotel and the associated park and waterfront areas.

Biscayne Boulevard Structures—PAST. In the 1930s, large hotels dominated downtown Miami's skyline along Biscayne Boulevard. The Miami Colonial Hotel is at the far left and the Everglades Hotel at the far right. Young Spanish-speaking women worked for the Miami Colonial Hotel as personal shoppers, happy to squire visitors to the finest shops. Hispanic tourists who had traveler's ailments had a choice of four physicians with Spanish surnames who advertised in tourist magazines. Residents at the 1929 Everglades Hotel had a camera view of Bayfront Park that often was better than a photograph. The rooftop pool deck had a breathtaking vista of downtown Miami and the Biscayne Bay. The 380-room Everglades was imploded January 22, 2005.

Biscayne Boulevard Structures—PRESENT. Today, Biscayne Boulevard separates Bayfront Park from the downtown Miami skyscrapers. Most of the hotels are gone.

View From Bayfront Park—PAST. A 1930s view of the McAllister and Columbus hotels from Bayfront Park.

View from Bayfront Park—PRESENT. The famous hotels along Biscayne Boulevard have been replaced with high-rise structures. Today, impressive skyscrapers like the 50 Biscayne Building (replaced the McAllister Hotel) and the Bank of America "New World Tower" (replaced the Columbus Hotel) dominate the western edge of Biscayne Boulevard.

McAllister Hotel—PAST. The McAllister Hotel, located on the northwest corner of Flagler Street and the Boulevard, was built in 1919. Across the Boulevard was the Elser Pier. The Royal Palm Park and Royal Palm Hotel were located south of the McAllister. The ten-story McAllister was Miami's largest — followed by the Biltmore Hotel in Coral Gables and the Royal Palm Hotel in downtown Miami — until the mid-1920s, when a skyline of tall buildings started to appear. The hotel, designed by Walter DeGarmo, was one of the city's most centralized, conveniently located near the shopping and theater districts and accessible to every resort attraction.

50 Biscayne—PRESENT. The McAllister Hotel was demolished in 1989 and replaced with the sleekly modern 50 Biscayne skyscraper building. In this view, west of 50 Biscayne, is the Alfred I. DuPont Building on Flagler Street.

Robert Clay Hotel—PAST. The Robert Clay Hotel was located within four blocks of Flagler Street, at 129 S.E. 4th Street in famous Fort Dallas Park, the most historic spot in South Florida. The Robert Clay had 164 rooms, each with a bath. The hotel, along with the neighboring Granada Apartments, Miami's first condominium, was torn down to make room for the Hyatt Hotel and Knight Center. The sender of this postcard in 1949 wrote: "It's cold here. Happy New Year—we are down for the Orange Bowl game."

Hyatt Hotel/Knight Center—PRESENT. The Hyatt Regency Hotel, located at 400 S.E. 2nd Avenue, was built next to the James L. Knight International Center (aka the Miami Convention Center). In addition to 615 regular rooms, there are over fifty units on the luxury Regency Club level, plus two lounges and two restaurants. Many of the rooms overlook the beautiful Miami River.

Leamington Hotel—PAST. The Leamington Hotel, located at 307 N.E. 1st Street, was opposite the Union Bus Station and overlooked Bayfront Park and the Biscayne Bay.

Leamington Hotel—PRESENT. The 100-room Leamington Hotel is still operating in downtown Miami.

Chapter Eight:

Leisure Activities and Attractions

Elser's Pier—PAST. Matthew Elser's Pier, which opened in 1917 at the foot of Flagler Street, was a recreation place for Miami's young people and tourists. The pier jutted out into Biscayne Bay. Here was a dance hall, shooting gallery, cotton candy, an exhibition hall, peep movie of hula dancers, and a photograph studio. The pier became downtown Miami's most popular venue for shopping and entertainment. The city of Miami purchased the pier in 1921; it was torn down in the mid-1920s when the Bayfront was filled to create Biscayne Boulevard and Bayfront Park.

Elser's Pier Site—PRESENT. The Elser's Pier site is now part of Bayfront Park. The area east of Flagler Street is a wide walkway leading to the fountain shown. Biscayne Bay is to the left in this view.

Pier 5—PAST. In the 1940s and 1950s, one of Miami's most popular tourist spots was the Pier 5 pier, with its distinctive neon sailfish. Pleasure boats and deep-sea fishing boats came and went. Here tickets were sold by barkers for sightseeing and fishing trips and glass-bottomed boat trips. People crowded the pier when the deep-sea fishing boats came in, bearing their catches of sailfish, barracuda, tarpon, marlin, and other game fish. A mechanically operated bulletin board was maintained for posting game-fish prizes. Nothing compares to the thrill of catching the big ones in the Gulf Stream, for amateur or professional.

Bayside Marketplace—PRESENT. Miami's famous Pier 5 commercial fishing pier with its neon sailfish sign is now gone, replaced by the Bayside Marketplace, an open-air shopping complex. Built in 1987 at 401 Biscayne Boulevard, the Bayside Marketplace is a sixteen-acre open-air mall and stage for concerts and theater. This 235,000-square-foot complex of two-story pavilions is home to around 175 commercial activities, including elegant shops, unique boutiques, fast food spots, fine restaurants, and stylish cafes. Locals and visitors flock to this popular bayfront complex to shop, dine, and enjoy the tropical ambiance and sometimes calypso and reggae music in the entertainment area. The marketplace is Miami's premier dining, shopping, and entertainment destination. Tour boat sightseeing cruises depart from the Marina (called the Miamorina) at Bayside.

Olympia Theater—PAST. White clouds and twinkling stars greeted the first audiences at the Olympic Theater when it opened its doors in 1926, at a cost of $1.5 million, as a silent movie house for Paramount Studios. The brick-faced theater is very ornate, resembling a courtyard with twinkling ceiling lights and rolling cloud puffs. People also were impressed with the theater's air conditioning, the first in the South. It was Florida's second largest theater. The theater's hidden lights reflected on its twisted columns and statues while clouds occasionally passed over a star-lit sky ceiling. Paul Whiteman accompanied the show with his 28-piece jazz orchestra. The Olympia Theater, located at 174 E. Flagler Street, seated over 2,000 patrons. The theater had a vaudeville show in addition to regular movies. One of the vaudeville performers was a young unknown, stand-up comic named Jackie Gleason. Hollywood stars Sarah Vaughn, Sophie Tucker, Eddie Cantor, Elvis Presley, Luciano Pavorotti and Gordon McRae were just a few of the big names to grace the stage. Its atmospheric architecture created the feeling of being in an Italian or Spanish villa courtyard. For many years the theater was the number one entertainment center in Miami. It was one of the last theaters in America to showcase vaudeville acts. Hard times closed its doors in 1954.

Gusman Center for the Performing Arts—PRESENT. South Florida business tycoon and philanthropist Maurice Gusman saved the aging theater and the adjacent Olympia Office Building from demolition and donated them to the City of Miami in 1975. The complex was renovated and renamed the Gusman Center for The Performing Arts in his honor. The vintage theater now has 1,700 seating capacity and a 65-foot-high royal blue night sky sprawling above the courtyard. Greek and Roman statues are framed by intricately carved columns and archways. The theater has a huge wow! Factor when you walk in. In 1988, The New World Symphony treated a Miami audience with an memorable debut performance. Music critics realized that Miami had converted a 1920s film palace into an elegant stage for performing arts. Today the Gusman Center is home to the Maximum Dance Company, the Florida Philharmonic Orchestra, the Miami International Film Festival, and the lobby serves as the Downtown Miami Welcome Center. The theater's ornate sidewalk ticket booth is still in use.

Vizcaya—PAST. In 1916, agricultural industrialist James Deering, carved a self-sufficient, seemingly antique Italian estate out of 180-acres of wild Florida he purchased from Mary Brickell. The 70-room Bayfront villa and its formal gardens became the winter retreat of the visionary Deering and his wealthy friends. Deering created an estate that looked as if an Italian family had lived in it for 400 years, with each generation adding its own period's furnishings. Deering named the estate, Vizcaya. The buildings at Vizcaya were designed by architect F. Burrel Hoffman Jr. and his associate Paul Chalfin. The gardens were the work of Diego Suarez. The historical estate is located at 3251 South Miami Avenue.

Vizcaya—PRESENT. In 1952, Dade County (now Miami-Dade County) purchased the estate from the Deering heirs for $1 million and opened it is a museum. With its unique architecture, gardens and interiors, this National Historic Landmark and European-inspired estate offers the perfect attraction for residents and visitors alike. Over 200,000 people visit this museum each year. Visitors feel as if they have been transported from New World to Old (no passport required). It is furnished just as it was in its early days, with a world-class decorative arts collection.

Deering Estate—PAST. Charles Deering (1852-1927), first chairman of the International Harvester Company and half-brother of Vizcaya owner James Deering, bought property consisting of an earlier home site and the Richmond College in 1913. In 1916, Deering remodeled the cottage and turned it into his private family home. Then in 1922, Deering constructed the Stone House, a 14,000-square-foot Mediterranean Revival style mansion. Deering died at the estate in 1927. The estate is located at 16701 S.W. 72nd Avenue.

Deering Estate—PRESENT. Deering relatives lived at the Deering Estate, the former winter home of Charles Deering, until 1980 and sold it in 1985 to the State of Florida and Miami-Dade County. It is now a history buff's dream and a county park with acres of virgin mangroves, palms, tropical hardwood hammock, and pineland. Deering's stone mansion and a timber-framed hotel, which was the original property on the estate, have been restored and open to the public. The estate reveals layers of South Florida's history — twentieth century, pioneer, and even prehistoric. Visitors may see the original site of the 1800s village of Cutler and a Tequesta Indian burial mound from around 1600.

Excursion Boats—PAST. Throughout the early part of the twentieth century, tour boats took tourists to attractions along the Biscayne Bay and Miami River. The excursion boats — including *Dixie, Lady Lou, Flamingo, Shamrock, Leo, Sallie,* and *Seminole Queen* — made stops at the popular attractions of Coppinger's Tropical Garden, Indian Village and Alligator Farm, and Musa Isle Seminole Indian Village. Shown is the Seven Seas *Dreamboat* that sailed daily out of Pier 10 in downtown Miami. The sender of the *Dreamboat* postcard wrote, "We took this boat trip today and it was grand. We saw two tribes of Indians and alligators & wild boars It was very nice and we enjoyed the trip." The Miami Beach *Show Boat* was the largest glass-bottom boat in the world and it enabled the passengers to behold the wonderful tropical undersea vegetation and fish on its pleasant trip around beautiful Biscayne Bay.

Excursion boats—PRESENT. The dockside at the Bayside Marketplace bustles with charter boats heading off on sightseeing trips around the Biscayne Bay. Shown are the *Island Queen* and *Tikki Beach* excursion boats. These boats offer passengers an excellent way of seeing Miami's fabulous skyline, Miami Beach, and the beautiful homes on Star, Palm, Hibiscus, and Fisher islands.

Miami Fronton—PAST. Jai-Alai was introduced to the United States in Miami in themed-1920s and has since flourished as one of the most exciting sports to watch. Pari-Mutuel wagering was allowed on the sport in 1934, and Jai-Alai became the only sport in the country where it was legal to bet on human beings.

Miami Fronton—PRESENT. Jai-Alai is a fascinating and dangerous game. The Miami Fronton, or arena, where the games are held, is the oldest in America and located just off N.W. 36th Street, east of the Miami International Airport. Today, in addition to Jai-Alai games, the fronton also allows players to participate in games of poker. It is great fun to watch Jai-Alai players whack around their pelata (ball) at lightning speed, and even more exciting to wager bets on who will win the game.

Alligator Wrestling in Miami—PAST. In 1919, John A. Roop opened Musa Isle Indian Village on the banks of the North Fork of the Miami River. The five-acre village included seven Indian houses or "chickees" with five Miccosukee Indian families in residence during the tourist season. Besides displaying typical Indian life and reptile and bird life, selling Indian crafts, alligator wrestling, Indian weddings, and other functions were staged here. Often the same couples were married more than once, but the tourists loved it.

Alligator Wrestling in Miami—PRESENT. The Miccosukee Indian Village is located on the Tamiami Trail west of Miami, in the Florida Everglades. Here Miccosukee Indians (a group of Seminole Indians) may be seen engaging in the art of bead-work, patchwork, basket weaving, woodwork, and doll making. The tribesmen perform live alligator demonstrations. Visitors can explore the Everglades on airboat rides, which pass through the untamed "River of Grass," and stop at an authentic, hammock-style Indian Camp that has been owned by the same Miccosukee family for over 100 years. The village also has a Museum of Indian artifacts, dioramas, photographs, and paintings.

Parrot Jungle—PAST. On December 20, 1936, Franz Scherr opened the Parrot Jungle to about 100 curious visitors, who paid a 25 cent admission to see twenty-five parrots and to listen to Scherr describe his small corner of paradise. Sixty-six years later, more than a thousand tropical birds and 2,000 plant varieties thrived at this popular Miami attraction. Colorful macaws free to fly as they please would often perch on a visitor's arm for pictures; they also performed tricks in the "Parrot Bowl." Parrot Jungle, located a few miles south of downtown Miami at 11000 S.W. 57th Avenue, was one of South Florida's unique bird sanctuary, wildlife habitat, and botanical garden. The attraction had trained bird and tropical wildlife shows. Parrot Jungle moved to a new location in 2003.

Jungle Island—PRESENT. After moving to Miami's Watson Island (a prime location off MacArthur Causeway) in 2003, the 18-acre Parrot Jungle was renamed Jungle Island and now stars birds, reptiles, and other animals, plus exhibits of orangutans, albino gators, and more. Visitors can see spectacular shows. There is an aviary fashioned after the clay cliffs in Peru, a replica of the Everglades environment with aquatic birds around a small lake and marsh, and a 2,000-pound crocosaurus. A 500-seat Serpentarium houses large reptiles and amphibians.

DC.283—Bulu, The Monkey Jungle's Famous Gorilla South of Miami, Fla.

Monkey Jungle—PAST. The Monkey Jungle, located at 14805 Southwest 216th Street in South Miami, is an attraction where the monkeys run free and humans are enclosed within cages. The attraction was born as a somewhat casual experiment with a release of primates into the wilds of Florida. The park was founded in 1933 by Joseph and Grace DuMond, who had raised monkeys in and around their former home in Connecticut. Based on their research, they purchased ten acres of Florida hardwood hammock that resembled a monkey habitat in Southeast Asia and released six crab-eating macaques into the woods and found they are very territorial. They began charging 10 cents to curious visitors who watched the wild monkeys from inside cages. In 1960, the DuMond family expanded the park with an Amazonian Rainforest that features South American monkeys living in a forest of native plants. The Monkey Jungle boasts the South's largest and one of America's most complete collections of monkeys and apes ranging from tiny Marmoset to Gorilla. The Monkey Jungle also contains one of the richest fossil deposits in southern Florida, with more than 5,000 specimens.

Monkey Jungle—PRESENT. Visitors experience mammals close to their hearts and genetic makeup while enjoying tropical rainforest at the Monkey Jungle. They witness monkeys swinging freely overhead or playing in the swimming area. The attraction is home to more than four hundred primates, representing thirty species. Gibbons, guenons, colobus, spider monkeys, and the tiny endangered Golden Lion Tamarin are just some of the primates visitors encounter.

Coral Castle—PAST. Coral Castle, a curious limestone mansion, located at 28655 S. Dixie Highway, was built by Edward Leedskalnin, a lovesick, five-foot-tall immigrant from Latvia. For nearly thirty years, Leedskalnin hauled huge blocks of coral onto his property. Using primitive homemade tools, he carved them into a house and furniture in tribute to a girlfriend who had jilted him back home. Its creator claimed to know the secret of the construction of the pyramids. Perhaps he did, for he was able to construct towers, massive stone furnishings, a nine-ton coral gate that swings open to the touch, a 5,000-pound valentine heart, and a myriad of other strange symbols of devotion to his mysterious lost love. Till this day, on one has ever figured out the builder's secret.

Coral Castle—PRESENT. The Coral Castle features the Heart Table, Moon Garden, the 25-foot-high Polaris Telescope, and the AC-Generator. Visitors can see Leedskalnin's coral bathtub, bed, reclining chair, a nine-ton gate, sundial, tables, and many symbols. This 1920s structure is considered one of the most remarkable achievements of modern times. Thirty-minute audio tours provide details of the castle in four languages, explaining the many interesting facts of Leedskalnin's life.

Hialeah Race Course—PAST. One of the first major tourist attractions of South Florida opened in 1925 at Hialeah Park. Each year, more than half a million people visited this magnificent track to thrill to its expansive, beautifully landscaped grounds and superb collection of wildlife. The 220-acre Hialeah Park boasted innumerable species of flowers, majestic trees and shrubs, architectural grandeur in the classic Mediterranean style and display of tropical birds and fish. From the clubhouse, Hialeah's famed flock of exotic, colorful flamingoes could be seen on their chosen island in the infield lake. Hialeah Race Course, the track that made Miami famous, was largely responsible for making Florida America's undisputed capital of winter horse racing.

Hialeah Race Course—PRESENT. For seventy-six years, the Hialeah Race Course was the winter mecca for the nation's finest horses and jockeys, the proving ground for the best three-year-old contenders for racing's Triple Crown and for all those who truly loved "the Sport of Kings." It was the world's most beautiful race course. Today the gates of Hialeah Park are closed and thoroughbred horse-racing at this once beautiful racetrack is no more. The last race was held May 22, 2001. The only horse at the track is the bronze statue of *Citation*. Major thoroughbred racing in Florida shifted to Gulfstream Park (now Gulfstream Gaming & Casino) in Hallandale, just north of Miami. The pink flamingoes still live in the track's infield. Listed on the National Register of Historic Places, the facilities at the park are now rented for social events.

Chapter Nine:
Key Biscayne

The seas, storms, and sands of a million years built the island known as Key Biscayne, located just southeast of downtown Miami. During the Ice Age, southern Florida sank below the sea and limestone was deposited over the submerged land. Then, as the limestone gradually rose above high tide, lower Florida and Key Biscayne were born. Drifting sands, carried by wind and water, covered the barren limestone island. The island grew — birds, insects, and animals arrived.

Primitive man's stay is known from two prehistoric Indian mounds found on the island by archaeologists in 1940. Bones of long extinct mammals were found on similar mounds in the area. Spanish explorer Juan Ponce de Leon was a Key Biscayne visitor in 1513. The Cape Florida Lighthouse was built in 1825 and remains one of the oldest structures in Florida. A temporary Army post, Fort Bankhead, was established here during the Second Seminole War. For a short while, pineapples were raised on the island.

In the 1880s pioneer Miamians regularly camped overnight on Key Biscayne. These hardy souls would leave the island at dawn and row to the edge of the Gulf Stream to hail passing ocean liners. Ships watched for the early Florida settlers and threw them "the current news" in the form of three-day-old New York newspapers in canvas sacks. Other early Miami residents regularly visited the island's wide beach to practice the popular sport of "Turtle turning." The helpless animals would be quickly butchered and the aroma of turtle chowder soon drifted over the island.

On November 9, 1947, the Rickenbacker Causeway opened, linking Key Biscayne with Miami. On hand at the opening ceremony was World War I flying ace, Captain Edward "Eddie" Rickenbacker. On that same day, the two northernmost miles of Key Biscayne became Crandon Park, which immediately became one of America's outstanding parks. The sprawling tropical paradise was named for Charles H. Crandon, who was the spark plug in making the causeway and park a reality. In 1951 the island had a post office, a community telephone, shopping center and residential housing development. In 1952, the magnificent Key Biscayne Hotel opened and tourism became the island's livelihood. Other motor hotels and restaurants followed, and the island was nicknamed "The Island Paradise."

On adjoining Virginia Key, between Key Biscayne and Miami, fifty-five bayside acres were transformed into the fabulous Miami Seaquarium. An outdoor zoo was established at Crandon Park. By 1955 the number of residents on Key Biscayne was over 3,000.

Six days after the 1960 presidential election, the Key was the site for a meeting unprecedented in American politics. President-elect John F. Kennedy came to the island to meet Vice President Richard M. Nixon at the Key Biscayne Hotel. Years later, Key Biscayne became a nationally recognized place name through the establishment of a satellite White House during the administration of President Richard M. Nixon (1969-1974).

Cape Florida Lighthouse—PRESENT. The Cape Florida Lighthouse still stands at the southern end of Key Biscayne. It is the oldest structure in South Florida. From its top iron parapet you can see downtown Miami with its modern glistening steel-glass towers — a contrast to the 95-foot-high lighthouse structure that has been restored by the Florida State Park Service. The Cape Florida Lighthouse is located in the Bill Baggs Florida State Recreation Area, a 406-acre spread of woods and beach named for a crusading Miami newspaper editor who campaigned for just such a sanctuary. There is more than a mile of beach for swimming, sunning, and fishing. Perched in the sand dunes, the 1825 lighthouse still peers across the horizon. The lighthouse was put on the National Register of Historic Places in 1971.

Cape Florida Lighthouse—PAST. Juan Ponce de Leon named this area "Cape of Florida" when he led the first Spanish expedition to Florida in 1513. The Cape Florida Lighthouse was completed in 1825, but was damaged during the Second Seminole War (1835-1842). It was rebuilt to its current 95-foot height after hurricane damage in 1855. The lighthouse has faithfully stood guard over the coast of South Florida for 185 years. Its beacon has guided sailors past Key Biscayne's treacherous sandbars and coral reefs, standing stalwart against hurricanes, Indian attacks, fire, Civil War battles, and environmental degradation.

Crandon Park—PAST. One of the loveliest parks in the Greater Miami area is Crandon Park. With a beach front of two miles and 10,000 coconut palms, waves purred gently against the beach. Dolphins and lovable Florida manatees were often seen swimming in the coastal waters. Leave it to the enterprising cameraman to gag the shot with gals. Here on the beach, only fifteen minutes from downtown Miami, visitors relaxed year-round. The land for the park was a gift from Dade County Commissioner Charles H. Crandon.

Crandon Park—PRESENT. The park's beautiful two-mile beach is consistently named among the top-ten beaches in America, celebrated for its pristine sand, calm water, winding promenade, and convenient amenities. A family amusement center includes a historic and restored carousel by the sea, picnic facilities, an old-fashioned, outdoor roller rink, and a host of marine play sculptures at the beach front playground. The park also has a world-class golf course and tennis center.

Miami Seaquarium—PAST. Founded in 1955, the Miami Seaquarium is one of the world's finest oceanariums dedicated to the research and preservation of sea life. Dolphins, killer whales, sharks, sea lions, manatees, and tropical fish are on display in the oceanarium on the Biscayne Bay at 4400 Rickenbacker Causeway. This 60-acre attraction is flanked by water on three sides and is home to 10,000 creatures of the sea.

Miami Seaquarium—PRESENT. The Miami Seaquarium is the longest-running tropical marine aquarium in the world, hosting over 600,000 visitors annually. A half-million gallon habitat, site of the park's amazing Dolphin Show, provides roomy confines for six Bottlenose Dolphins. These animals can be viewed any time through 126 viewing windows. It is the only place in the world where Pacific dolphins perform alongside three-ton Killer Whales. Visitors especially enjoy Lolita, the Killer Whale; Flipper, the Atlantic Bottlenose Dolphin; giant sharks patrolling their territory, and slithery moray eels lurking in coral reef caverns. The Seaquarium has a Sea Lion Show, Killer Whale Show, shark tanks, bird exhibits, rainforest, an Everglades' exhibit, and a monorail system that connects the various areas.

Chapter Ten:

More Faces of Miami

Ancient Spanish Monastery—PAST. Noted publisher William Randolph Hearst searched the world over for art treasures. In 1925, he discovered and purchased for $500,000 a long-forgotten Spanish Monastery, which, in 1835, had been confiscated by the Spanish Government and sold to a farmer to store grain. The twelfth century monastery was operated by the Cistercian Order for 694 years. Hearst had intended to transport the architectural gem to his estate in San Simeon, California. The more than 36,000 heavy pieces were packed in some 10,751 crates and shipped to New York. There they were stored and not moved because of the Depression. In the 1950s, two Ohio businessmen bought the Monastery and reassembled it in North Miami. It took nineteen months and cost $1.5 million to rebuild the structure at 16711 West Dixie Highway. The Monastery, situated in a formal Spanish garden, contains priceless Middle Age artifacts and is open to the public. The monastery regained a religious function in 1964 when it became owned by the Episcopalian Church.

St. Bernard de Clairvaux Episcopal Church and the Ancient Spanish Monastery—PRESENT. St. Bernard's Church, as it is known today, started out not on the monastery grounds, but at a savings and loan building on N.E. 167th Street as "The Mission of St. John the Divine," eventually becoming the Church of St. Bernard de Clairvaux. Later, a benefactor of many Episcopal churches purchased the monastery and presented it to the parish of St. Benard de Clairvaux. The monastery contains notable antiques and works of art, and there are six acres of formal gardens. Now church services are held on Sunday; it is also a popular oasis, especially for weddings.

The Torch of Friendship—PAST. Miami is the gateway to Latin America and has strong ties with our neighbors to the South. The people of Miami wanted to create a tangible sign of good will and lasting friendship to let the world know its warm feeling for Pan America. So the attractive Torch of Friendship monument was erected in 1960 on beautiful palm-lined Biscayne Boulevard in Bayfront Park. The monument features the flags and great seals of Caribbean and Latin American countries; the ever-burning Torch symbolizes inter-American friendship and understanding. Natural gas provides fuel for the flame, which burns continuously. Native stone quarried from the Florida Keys was used in the construction of both the shaft and the forty-foot-long curved stone wall. After the assassination of President John F. Kennedy in 1963, the monument was dedicated to the memory of the late President.

The Torch of Friendship—PRESENT. The John F. Kennedy Torch of Friendship in Bayfront Park is a symbol of the close relations that prevail between Miami and the Latin republics to the south. It has become a popular gathering place for memorials, protests, and rallies. The gap in the plaques around the memorial is for Cuba, which will be added at the demise of the communist Castro regime.

Barnacle House—PAST. The Barnacle House, located at 3485 Main Highway in Coconut Grove, was built by Massachusetts-born naval architect Ralph Middleton Munroe in 1891. Munroe purchased forty acres of bayside land in Coconut Grove, which at that time lacked even a road link to Miami and created the Barnacle from wood salvaged from shipwrecks. To improve air circulation and avoid flooding, Munroe raised the house eight feet above ground, vented the roof, and covered the porch to enable windows to be opened during storms. These and a host of other unique features made life bearable in the hot and humid south Florida summers. When the family grew, Munroe simply jacked up the first floor to become the second and built a new floor underneath. He also built a semi-attached one-story library. Privacy was ensured by the hardwood forest "hammock" between the house and the highway, through which Munroe cleared a path just wide enough for one buggy.

Barnacle House—PRESENT. Commodore Munroe lived in the house until his death in 1933, and his descendants occupied it until 1973, when they sold it to the State of Florida so a portion of old Florida could be preserved. Today, the Barnacle, one of Miami's most treasured landmarks, is an historic state park. It is listed on the National Register of Historic Places. It is also the oldest house in Miami-Dade County to remain on its original site.

Miami Book Fair International—PAST. In downtown Miami the Miami International Book Fair attracts distinguished authors, droves of avid readers, and book collectors from all over the world, to the tune of half a million visitors. It has become the leading such event in the nation. The book fair, which started in 1984, is held on the streets by the Miami-Dade Community College, Wolfson Campus, 300 N.E. Second Avenue, in downtown Miami.

Miami Book Fair International—PRESENT. Touted as the preeminent literary gathering of its kind, the Miami International Book Fair is a week-long celebration of the written word, with star authors chronicling their works in a series of readings and lectures. This premier celebration of books features titles and authors from South American and the Caribbean Islands as well as the U.S. In 2008, the event featured over 350 authors, a street fair, 200 exhibitors, Children's Alley, and Comix Galaxy.

Historical Museum of Southern Florida—PAST. Located at 101 West Flagler Street and part of the Metro-Dade Cultural Center, the Historical Museum of Southern Florida was designed by Philip Johnson. This museum takes a sweeping look at 10,000 years of history in Southern Florida. Visitors can explore the past along a pathway of human progress, with thematic and visiting exhibits highlighting special topics.

Historical Museum of Southern Florida—PRESENT. The museum has a variety of interactive environments including a Spanish fort, a Seminole Indian chickee, an early homesteader's cottage, a 1920s trolley car, and a nineteenth century sailboat. On permanent display is a history of South Florida. The 10,000-square-foot museum contains hundreds of artifacts, dioramas, photographs, interactive displays, a research center, and a large gift shop.

Opa-Locka City Hall—PAST. Glenn H. Curtiss, a former pioneer airman turned urban developer, created the planned town of Opa-Locka, just north of Miami, to evoke an "Arabian fantasy" based on the book *1001 Tales of the Arabian Nights*. Streets were laid out in Moorish Crescent patterns, and the multi-domed City Hall was the community's centerpiece. Pink stripes, pink domes, minarets, and giant pink urns link the 1920s building to Miami's famed Art Deco tradition.

Opa-Locka City Hall—PRESENT. An exotic and glamorous design, the entire city of Opa-Locka was originally planned to be modeled on the Arabian nights theme, but time, the tides, the military, and other changes have had a less than a positive effect, and the city is now working hard to overcome some of the negative perceptions that it has been burdened with. The City Hall, which was restored in 1987, is the centerpiece of the Opa-Locka Moorish architecture. The City Hall is listed on the National Register of Historic Places, along with twenty other buildings in Opa-Locka.

Everglades—PAST. The Florida Everglades, west of Miami, occupy a nearly level plain that slopes from fifteen-feet above sea level at the southern shore of Lake Okeechobee to sea level at the tip of the peninsula. Covering 4,472 square miles, it is by far the most extensive swampland in the United States. *Pay-hai-o-kee*, meaning grass-water, is what the Seminole Indians call it and, for the most part, that is what it is. The whole drowned plain is blanketed with tall growths of sawgrass, and differs from most swamps in that trees are generally confined to small clumps or islands.

Everglades—PRESENT. The Everglades used to cover more than one-quarter of the entire state of Florida, but much of the land has been filled in to prevent flooding caused by hurricanes and, later, for development purposes. What remains is a 200-mile-long, 50-mile-wide, and on average, 6" deep "river of grass." The water flows from the Kissimmee River Valley in central Florida to Florida Bay and the Atlantic Ocean. The wildest of Florida's wildlife still roam in the Everglades. The Everglades' most famous resident is the alligator. Other inhabitants include crocodiles, Florida panthers, green sea turtles, deer, and a wide variety of birds. The deer shown was photographed in 2005 during a trip into the Everglades.

Part III:
Miami Beach Past and Present

Chapter Eleven:
Around the City

Miami Beach had its beginning as a coconut plantation. The plantation owners Elnathan T. Field and Ezra Osborn purchased the land from the government for less than an average of $1.30 per acre.

The first house on Miami Beach was built by Charles M. Lum in 1866. Up until 1913, the only way to reach Miami Beach was by boat. A ferryboat connected the Beach with Miami, docking at what is now Biscayne Boulevard and SE First Street.

John S. Collins, a merchant from Moorestown, New Jersey, first became interested in Miami Beach in the 1890s. He visited Miami Beach at that time by hiring a rowboat to take him across the Biscayne Bay. Having been raised on a farm, he was first interested because of the rich soil and was convinced that a profitable farming venture could be started, with the idea of selling the winter produce to the northern visitors who were flocking to Miami during the cold winter months.

In 1907, Collins purchased the Osborne property and became associated with Elnathan T. Field. Miami Beach at that time consisted of mangrove swamps and palmetto scrub. Ten acres were finally cleared and planted in avocados, but the crop was a failure. Field became disgusted and sold out to Collins, who now was the sole owner of 1,670 acres of land along the oceanfront. Undaunted by his first failure, he kept on trying, and soon had the largest plantation of its kind, raising tomatoes, potatoes and other garden vegetables, bananas, mango trees and an assortment of tropical fruits. He found a ready market across Biscayne Bay.

In 1911, Collins decided that a cheaper way must be found to move his products to market. Collins and his son-in-law, Thomas J. Pancoast, formed a joint venture and completed the Collins Canal that runs from Lake Pancoast to Biscayne Bay. Work was then started on a causeway to Miami, and in 1913, a wooden toll bridge, the Collins Causeway, was opened. The bridge was the impetus needed to start Miami Beach on its way as the resort capital of the western world. It was a turning point for Miami Beach.

The next person to become interested in this tropical beach was Carl Graham Fisher from Indianapolis, Indiana. Fisher and one of his closest friends, James A. Allison, also of Indianapolis, had incorporated and amassed a fortune from the Presto-O-Lite Company.

Fisher visited Miami and was so enchanted with the city that he bought a home here to settle down and enjoy a good vacation. Fisher supplied John S. Collins with sufficient money for Collins to finish his bridge, receiving two hundred acres of beach land in return. He then purchased an additional two hundred acres of beach land and sixty acres on the bay front. In 1913, Fisher returned to Indianapolis and left his friend, John Levi in charge of his holdings, which was then known as the Alton Beach Property. Up until this time about two-thirds of what is now Miami Beach was covered by mangroves and under water at high tide. Fisher's company added six million cubic yards of "fill" to cover 1,000 acres and topped this fill with soil from the Everglades. Grass was sown and trees, plants, and shrubs transplanted, which created the Venetian-like beauty that exists to this day with lakes and waterways and also separates and slices Miami Beach into islands. Fisher reclaimed an additional 2,760 acres, using 14.3 million cubic yards of fill. These holdings extended along the bay front from the southern tip to a point approximately six miles north.

On March 26, 1915, Miami Beach was incorporated as a township. It covered the area Government Cut, the ship channel to 42nd Street. Two years later, on May 21, 1917, Miami Beach was incorporated as a city. Miami Beach thus was born a city destined to push aside shortsighted critics and become the nation's No. 1 playground, in the land of perpetual summer.

The Miami Beach Bayshore Company, a new Carl Fisher enterprise, was formed in 1918, and soon became the owner of 1,600 acres to the north of the active developments. This land was filled, streets were laid out and paved, trees and shrubbery planted.

With all this new man-made land, real estate values increased by leaps and bounds. Fisher built his own power plant and the island now had electricity. Next Fisher built hotels, golf courses, public parks and many other improvements. Miami Beach was beginning to look like a resort. The main arteries of traffic were Collins Avenue, Alton Road and a few cross streets. Fisher built the Lincoln, Flamingo and Nautilus hotels. He then built the Nautilus Polo Field and imported polo players from Europe, paying them $15,000 a year each, to show Americans how it was done.

During World War II, soldiers found Miami Beach a near perfect environment for training, and then respite from combat zone prior to reassignment. Between 1942 and 1945, one-fifth of all enlisted men and one-fourth of all officers in the Army Air Force trained in Miami Beach — over a half-million men and women. The United States Army leased more than two hundred hotels. At war's end, many of these ex-soldiers, having gotten sand in their shoes, eventually settled in this tropical paradise. In the 1940s, writing for the Miami Herald, Laurence Schwab wrote:

> "The narrow strip of island which in peacetime is a reasonable facsimile of heaven, is one of the largest non-flying bases of the Army Air Corps. The Officers Training School is now popularly known as Camp Roney Plaza, as its activities are centered around that plush resort hotel. In six short weeks, civilians are changed into ground officers for aviation… golf courses that, a few months ago, echoed to irritated 'fores' now are pounded daily by thousands of feet. Military public speaking is taught in a former beauty parlor by the Roney Plaza pool deck. Officer candidate school members are selected by merit… and their course lasts 12 weeks."

Miami Beach is a unique city, with no cemetery, no railroad, no airport, and manufacturing was not allowed. In 1951, there were almost 5,000 residents, over 360 hotels with over 26,000 rooms, over 1,500 apartment houses with over 16,000 units, and, in this year, there were only four days on which the sun did not shine. The city had three golf courses, thirteen theaters, two hospitals, thirteen city parks, five commercial banks/federal savings associations, fifteen churches, six public schools, and fifty private schools.

Many are under the impression that Miami Beach is a part of Miami. This, however, is untrue; Miami Beach is a separate municipality with a city manager form of government.

Modern-day South Beach (SoBe) is a vibrant monument to the Art Deco designs of the 1930s. The narrow streets are lined with buildings designed with curved edges, porthole windows, and pastel-colored facades — all touchstones of the style. Some of the small hotels have horizontal banding and "eyebrows," which are cantilevered sunshades located over exterior windows that create interesting shadows on the façade of the structure. Everywhere you look there is an echo, an allusion, to this most instantly recognizable decorative style, even in the colors and shapes of the South Beach lifeguard towers.

There are some eight hundred edifices in the Art Deco style. Most of the beachfront properties are still hotels, but some have been converted into condos or apartment hotels. The Miami Design Preservation League offers tours of the Art Deco Historic District. The pastel colors of Art Deco architecture radiate in the bright South Beach sun. Mega-hotels have elbowed in alongside the pastel Art Deco properties that give this small enclave its color and tropical charm. A stroll through the Art Deco District of South Beach is a return trip to the 1930s.

Miami Beach—PAST. Carl Fisher and his gang of dredgers scooped up sand from the bottom of the Biscayne Bay, challenged the supremacy of the mangrove tangles off the coast of a newborn town called Miami, and created something far greater than he knew — the first modern "resort," destined to stand as a model for all the Winter Playgrounds and Capitals of Sun and Fun that came later.

Miami Beach—PRESENT. There is only one Miami Beach. It is unique. It has sunny skies, marvelous weather, sea kissed breezes, sandy beaches, world class resorts, museums, golf courses, and the world's biggest and most eye-opening collection of 1920s/1930s architecture and decoration, not behind glass, but a living, breathing eighty-block monument to the Art Deco era. In this view is Fisher Island on the left and Miami Beach on the right.

City Hall—PAST. The Old Miami Beach City Hall, located at 1130 Washington Avenue, was constructed in 1927, after the devastating hurricane of 1926. The structure was designed by architect Martin L. Hampton. The building was designed with Beaux Arts and Mediterranean details. Prominent Mediterranean motifs are the red tile hipped roofs and the Italian Renaissance balusters and urns. The two-story horizontal structure forms the base for a nine-story tower that is located at the center of the base structure.

Old City Hall Building—PRESENT. The Old City Hall building has column-studded corridors that brood with history. After construction of a new City Hall building in 1975, on 17th Street, near the Miami Beach Convention Center, the Old City Hall structure was renovated in 1987. For a short while the Old City Hall was used as the Miami Beach campus of the University of Miami; now it houses court facilities and offices.

Miami Beach Post Office—PAST. Miami Beach's post office, designed by Howard L. Chesney and built by President Franklin D. Roosevelt's Works Progress Administration (WPA), which hired not only skilled artisans, but also unskilled workers and trained them on the job. Located at 1300 Washington Avenue, the structure is an "L" shaped building with the entrance at the corner of the L that is dominated by a rotunda. The circular structure is flanked on either side by lower rectangular masses. The roof of the rotunda is topped by a lantern.

Miami Beach Post Office—PRESENT. Tourists to Miami Beach enjoy sending their family and friends postcards from this Art Deco gem, the first South Beach renovation project tackled by preservationists in the 1970s. The Miami Beach Post Office is an excellent example of Deco Federal, an architectural style that evolved during the Federal Government's building program of the Depression. Classical motifs and subdued decoration distinguished the post office from the neighboring Art Deco buildings. Within the rotunda, housing the public area, are original stamp tables and mailboxes and an eye-catching mural by Charles Hardin, showing scenes of Cavalry and Indians, fills one wall. On the exterior there is a bald eagle over the entrance.

Miami Beach Convention Center—PAST. Although Miami Beach is noted for its "fun in the sun" way of life, it is also known as a destination for conventioneers. The Miami Beach Convention Center is located at 1901 Convention Center Drive (between Washington Avenue and 17th and 19th streets). The Convention Hall, with an overall floor area of 200,000 square feet, seated 15,000 persons, and the interior could be arranged to provide for more than 700 exhibition booths. The hall has been used for such widely varying purposes as conventions, trade shows, the circus, and boxing matches. Adjoining Convention Hall was the Municipal Auditorium, with seating for 3,600. On February 25, 1964, Cassius Clay fought Sonny Liston for the heavyweight boxing championship of the world in the Auditorium. After he won the title, he proclaimed his new name — Muhammad Ali. At times the facilities of both buildings were combined, thereby providing 173,000 square feet of exhibit space and 1,039 booths.

Miami Beach Convention Center—PRESENT. In 1988, the Miami Beach Convention Center opened with 1.1-million-square feet of exhibition space. It also got a striking new façade that has often been praised as a compendium of Art Deco styles.

Jackie Gleason Theater of the Performing Arts—PAST. Located at 1700 Washington Avenue, the theater was designed in 1950-51 by three of the most familiar names among Art Deco architecture: Henry Hohauser, Russell Pancoast, and L. Murray Dixon. From September 1964 until 1970, "The Jackie Gleason Show," with its highly stylized vaudeville-like shenanigans, aired once a week. More than 40 million people tuned in to watch. The show was an invaluable publicity boom for Miami Beach. For several years, Gleason was the self-proclaimed "King of Miami Beach."

Fillmore Miami Beach at Jackie Gleason Theater—PRESENT. Better known as the Jackie Gleason Theater, this renovated, light-blue Deco beauty is a wonderful facility for traveling Broadway shows and classical musical concerts. The theater can seat 3,000 people; a Roy Lichtenstein *Mermaid* sculpture graces the front lawn of the theater.

Miami Beach Public Library and Art Center—PAST. The John S. Collins Memorial Library, designed by Russell T. Pancoast, grandson of Miami Beach pioneer John A. Collins, was built in 1931 on property presented to the city for a public park (Collins Park). The library, which had approximately 50,000 volumes, was maintained by the City of Miami Beach. The Collins Library, located at 2121 Park Avenue, was later used as the core of the Bass Museum of Art.

Bass Museum of Art—PRESENT. The City of Miami Beach built a new Public Library in 1963 and philanthropists John and Johanna Bass donated the money for the renovation of the building and for an art collection to be housed in the building, which was renamed the Bass Museum of Art. The museum, in the heart of the historic Art Deco District, offers an overview of major European paintings, sculpture, and textiles, plus temporary exhibitions of contemporary art from around the world. Its permanent collection, spanning more than 500 years and four continents, is the most varied in the region. Enormous African baobab trees are in front of the historic structure. The museum's original 1930s building was expanded in 2002 by renowned architect Arata Isozaki. The structure is on the National Register of Historic Places.

Miami Beach Kennel Club—PAST. This ocean-front kennel club contributed to a pleasure-packed winter season at Miami Beach with the "finest in dog racing" each weekday night. Good dogs and champions from top ranking kennels kept the competition keen; every night's program spiritedly interesting. At night, with the cry "There goes Lucky," the speeding mechanical rabbit set the lithe, powerful dogs off. The speed and heart of these greyhounds, trained in racing, is amazing. All racing and mutuels at the Miami Beach Kennel Club were under the supervision of the state racing commission. Ladies, attired in fine dresses and gloves, and men, in suits and ties, relaxed with a cocktail in the glass-enclosed Clubhouse or enjoyed the sea air from the Grandstand. Dog handlers decked out in Bahamian-style military uniforms paraded the greyhounds down the track. Other entertainments enticed patrons elsewhere over the years and the Kennel Club fell on hard times. The dog track, with its private 300-foot beach, was torn down as part of assembling the land for the original South Shore redevelopment project and faded into history. The South Pointe Towers and South Pointe Park now stands on the site.

South Pointe Towers and Park—PRESENT. Located on the southern top of Miami Beach are the South Pointe Towers and South Pointe Park. The seventeen-acre park is a popular recreational spot with a nice beach, areas landscaped with tropical palms, and wide walkways. Beside the park are several ultra-modern tower condominium structures.

Chapter Twelve:

Street Scenes

Popular streets in Miami Beach include Collins Avenue, Lincoln Road, Espanola Way, Ocean Drive, Alton Road, and Washington Avenue. Collins Avenue (Highway A1A) runs north and south along the Atlantic Ocean. It was named after John Collins, one of the first pioneers of Miami Beach. He was a farmer and land developer who first grew coconuts on Miami Beach and built the first wooden bridge connecting Miami and Miami Beach. Lincoln Road was named after Carl Fisher's (developer of Miami Beach) favorite president, Abraham Lincoln.

County Causeway—PAST. The County Causeway (later became MacArthur Causeway) connects Miami and Miami Beach. The eastern end of the causeway becomes Fifth Street at the southern end of Miami Beach; the western end of the causeway starts in downtown Miami. The causeway offers a good view of cruise ships entering or leaving the Port of Miami.

MacArthur Causeway—PRESENT. During World War II, the Dade County (now Miami-Dade County) Commission honored the defender of Bataan, General Douglas MacArthur, by renaming the County Causeway. The MacArthur Causeway is where the popular movie "True Lies," with Arnold Schwarzennegger and Jamie Lee Curtis, was filmed. In this view is the eastern end of MacArthur Causeway as it approaches Miami Beach. A cruise ship is in the channel leading to the Atlantic Ocean.

South Miami Beach—PAST. The southern end of Miami Beach has been the bathing place for residents of Miami since the early 1900s. The popular beach in South Miami Beach was (and still is) Lummus Park, which borders Ocean Drive from 6th Street to 14th Lane. The park was a veritable paradise for those who visited it for a swim in the surf or merely to stroll through the tropical foliage. On the west side were scores of fine hotels overlooking the park and the pulsing Atlantic Ocean.

South Miami Beach—PRESENT. At the southern end of Miami Beach is the fascinating Art Deco District, designated a historic district in 1979 by the National Register of Historic Places. The district includes more than 800 buildings, many of which have been restored. The eclectic architectural styles include Art Deco, Streamline Modern, and Spanish Mediterranean Revival with tropical motifs and colors. The flamboyant buildings are painted in beautiful pastels: salmon and flamingo pinks, lavender, turquoise, powder blue, seafoam green, steel gray, sunny yellow, and racing stripes. Today the area is also a late-night hot spot with a hip after-hours scene. Lummus Park and Beach is even more popular now than it was in the 1930s or 1940s.

Ocean Drive and Lummus Park—PAST. In the mid-1930s, Miami Beach came out of the Great Depression by experiencing a tremendous building boom. Between 1935 and 1940 alone, almost two hundred new hotels and apartments were built on the beach in the new modern architectural style. Today, seventy years later, many of them remain as the Art Deco gems of South Beach.

Ocean Drive and Lummus Park—PRESENT. Today Ocean Drive is America's great cruising strip — an endless parade of classic cars, pretty girls and handsome guys, street performers, vendors, celebrities pretending to be tourists and tourists who want to play celebrity, and ugly people and beautiful people. On any given day there could be an alligator strolling Ocean Drive for a documentary film, a woman riding on a horse for a soft drink ad, a lion lounging on the beach surrounded by beautiful models, or stunt people throwing themselves through windows.

Traffic on Ocean Drive—PAST. In 1930, the automobile traffic on Ocean Drive was moderate.

Traffic on Ocean Drive—PRESENT. Today, the Art Deco hotels and popular restaurants and nightclubs in South Beach have helped increase the automobile traffic on Ocean Drive.

Collins Avenue—PAST. Collins Avenue, named in honor of Miami Beach pioneer John S. Collins, is a thoroughfare that runs the entire length of Miami Beach through the heart of what was once a large fruit grove and vegetable farm. Beginning with the southern part of this famous street are business establishments, apartments, and moderately priced hotels. Farther north the street makes rapid changes — from business districts to luxurious resort hotels. In the 1950s, if you were to drive the entire length of the avenue, you could count almost two hundred hotels, not to mention apartments and guest houses. The hotels varied from fifteen rooms to around 550, with rates ranging from $2 to $50 per day.

Collins Avenue—PRESENT. Collins Avenue has more hotels than any street of comparable length in the world. Larger hotels are located on the ocean side of Collins Avenue; smaller hotels on the western side.

Collins Avenue and Lincoln Road—PAST. Looking north on Collins Avenue from Lincoln Road are the DeLano, National, Sagamore, and DiLido hotels.

Collins Avenue and Lincoln Road—PRESENT. Looking north on Collins Avenue from Lincoln Road are the Park Central, DeLano, National, and the northwest corner of Sagamore hotels.

Lincoln Road—PAST. In 1905, woodsmen gathering mangrove bark for tannic acid cleared a wide path from the ocean to the bay; years later, it was widened, paved, and became known as "The Most Beautiful Shopping Lane in the World" and "The Fifth Avenue of the South." The business district of this thoroughfare is only nine blocks long; however, it represented more prominent mercantile establishments than any other street in the South. Architect Morris Lapidus, who designed many of the Miami Beach hotels, designed several structures on Lincoln Road, including the Sterling Building, Lincoln Theater, and Colony Theater. In this view is the F. W. Woolworth Store on the left and the Depression Modern style Post Office on the right.

Lincoln Road Mall—PRESENT. In 1960, the city hired Morris Lapidus to design new landscaping for the pedestrian-only street, now called the Lincoln Road Mall, which stretches from Washington Avenue to Alton Road. Certainly one of the world's most picturesque shopping areas, Lincoln Road Mall combines the charm of tropical patio with the intrigue of the latest fashions. In each block along the mall are shelters where shoppers may rest with palms, flower beds, and foliage all but masking the display windows of shops along each side of a broad walkway. Fountains and reflection pools add to the atmosphere. Business houses along the mall range from theaters and exclusive specialty shops to trendy watering holes, sidewalk cafes, and galleries. The Miami Beach Community Church (500 Lincoln Road), built in 1921, the city's first church, is still here. The mall is a popular place for locals to see and be seen.

Fisher's Office Building—PAST. Pioneering Miami Beach developer Carl Fisher built the seven-story Mediterranean office building on Lincoln Road in 1924. He used the building to bring prospective property owners to the top floor to scout their building sites.

Van Dyke Building—PRESENT. Carl Fisher's Office Building, now the Van Dyke, houses a popular restaurant and jazz bar.

Washington Avenue—PAST. Washington Avenue was the principal business (or Main Street) thoroughfare of Miami Beach, with nationally known 5 and 10 cent stores, groceries, hotels, chain stores, markets, apartments, theaters, post office, "Spanish Village," City Hall, and travel bureaus. The avenue, two blocks west of the ocean, was once the trolley route to Miami.

Washington Avenue—PRESENT. Washington Avenue has undergone many changes since the 1930s; however, it is still one of the busiest streets in Miami Beach.

Espanola Way—PAST. Espanola Way, designed as a "Spanish Village" in 1922, is located between 14th and 15th streets west of Washington Avenue. The narrow street was unlike any other in Miami Beach — an intimate thoroughfare with the feel of old Madrid. Red barrel-tile roofs, arches, and balconies with wrought-iron railings added to the Mediterranean look. Desi Arnaz was introduced to the American audience in a restaurant on this street. The Clay Hotel (shown in the center) stood at the entrance to Espanola Way. During prohibition, it was a gambling and bootlegging den and the headquarters for mobster Al Capone's gambling syndicate.

Espanola Way—PRESENT. This narrow street — a lovely haven of multi-hued Mediterranean buildings with gleaming white buttresses and gas lamps — was first envisioned as an artist's colony. The boutiques, art galleries, charming restaurants, and off-beat shops make it perfect for window shopping, art browsing, people watching, and café sipping. With a little imagination, visitors to the Clay Hotel (on the left) can experience a night in Europe. Europeans visiting here will feel right at home. If one visits Rooms 128-138 in the Clay Hotel, they can even imagine what Al Capone's 1930s gambling casino might have looked like.

Chapter Thirteen:

At the Beach

Sun, Gorgeous Beach, and Palm Trees—PAST. People of all ages in the early twentieth century went to the beach for a day of fun and relaxation. Sunning, splashing in the water, and building sand castles were popular activities for the residents and visitors in this 1920s Miami Beach scene. Note the woolen bathing suits. The bathers' attire led one observer to comment: "There wasn't much white meat, but there was lots of dressing."

Sun, Gorgeous Beach, and Palm Trees—PRESENT. Today, sun worshipers still dot the miles of golden sand at Miami Beach. Going to the beach has always been a great American pastime. However, in later years the bathing suits became bikinis and brevity would be the norm for most young ladies. The young men and women that go to the beach today wouldn't be caught dead in an early twentieth century woolen bathing suit.

Lummus Park and Beach—PAST. Lummus Park, located on Ocean Drive between 6th Street and 14th Lane, is not to be confused with the Lummus Park in Miami. This stretch of the celebrated Miami Beach was one of the few beaches open to the public. The park extends to the coconut palm shaded beach where thousands enjoyed the breakers and vivid blue waters of the Atlantic Ocean. This was a favorite spot for sun bathing, surf bathing, tanned torsos, colorful umbrellas, and for picnicking on the grounds among the palms. The park is named after the first Mayor of Miami Beach, J. N. Lummus, who sold the city the property with the stipulation that it could never be used for commercial purposes, and that it was to be used as a public park only. One of the finest natural beaches located on Miami Beach it has a wide expanse of fine golden sand, and is a tropical paradise of graceful leaning coconut palms. It is used primarily by visitors to the area for sun and surf bathing. In the first half of the twentieth century, Lummus Park was one of the most popular beaches in the Greater Miami area.

Lummus Park and Beach—PRESENT. Lummus Park is now the most popular beach in South Beach (SoBe). The long expanse of immaculate sandy beach and palm trees is located in the now popular South Miami Beach Art Deco area. The swaying coconut palm trees filter the sunshine for beach-goers that enjoy the shade.

Walking Among the Palms—PAST. Lummus Park in South Miami Beach was the only stretch of Miami Beach where no buildings blocked the view of the ocean from the road (Ocean Drive). With swaying coconut palm trees, this beach walkway provided an unmistakable impression of the South Seas.

Walking Among the Palms—PRESENT. Today, there is a wavy Lummus Beach promenade sandwiched between the beach and Ocean Drive that extends from 6th Street to 14th Lane. The picturesque walkway is lined with coconut palms and other subtropical plants.

South Beach Lifeguard Stations—PAST. In this 1950s view of Miami Beach the lifeguard stations were plain simple structures.

South Beach Lifeguard Stations—PRESENT. Today, colorful Art Deco lifeguard stations stretch along the ocean from South Pointe to 85th Street. The stations, which vary in colors and shapes, provide beach-goers with interesting art objects to enjoy.

Southern Tip of Miami Beach—PAST. In early twentieth century, the Miami Beach Kennel Club was located on the southeastern tip of Miami Beach. This gaming attraction was torn down and replaced with South Pointe Park (shown here). Just north of the park are the hotels and beach along Ocean Drive.

Southern Tip of Miami Beach—PRESENT. South Pointe Park offers an ideal vantage point to watch luxury cruise ships make their way out to sea. The park is a veritable paradise for those who visit it for a swim in the surf or merely to stroll through the tropical foliage. Located north of the park are several modern condominium towers.

Chapter Fourteen:

Hotels in the Art Deco Area

South Beach

Hotels Along Ocean Drive

Breakwater Hotel—PAST. The 59-room Breakwater Hotel, located at 940 Ocean Drive, was designed by Anton Skistewiczs and built in 1939. A memorable feature of the hotel is its vertical tower, with double-faced signage in blue neon that glows afar at night. The hotel is noted for its roof deck and the Neptune mosaic at the bottom of the swimming pool. The roof deck is surrounded by a railing that would be at home on any of the cruise ships that sail out of the Port of Miami.

Breakwater Hotel—PRESENT. The streamline-styled Breakwater Hotel is located in the heart of Miami Beach's historic Art Deco district and puts hotel visitors right in the middle of the South Beach action. The restored hotel has flamingos and palm trees etched on the glass of the lobby windows and are fine examples of the tropical imagery that architects integrated into their designs. The hotel became part of fashion in 1986 when the rooftop location was used as a background for fashion models posing for perfume ads. In late 2009, when this picture was taken, the hotel was closed and undergoing modification.

Cardoza Hotel—PAST. The Cardoza Hotel, located at 1300 Ocean Drive, was designed by architect Henry Hohauser and built in 1939. This 44-room, Streamline Moderne hotel includes classic features such as neon, curves, and eyebrows (shades over the windows). The keystone façade is a classic of Streamline design. Named after the 1930s Supreme Court Justice Benjamin Cardoza, the hotel was used as a set for the Frank Sinatra movie "A Hole in the Head" in 1959.

Cardoza Hotel—PRESENT. The hotel faded badly in the 1960s and 1970s, but was the first to be renovated by Barbara Capitman's son Andrew during South Beach's revival in the 1980s. The exterior and rooms have been beautifully redone. It is a landmark South Beach hotel now owned by the two people most responsible for the Latin pop explosion, Gloria and Emilio Estefan. Downstairs is Oriente restaurant, with a kind of upscale Cuban-Chinese aesthetic. Upstairs are deluxe views of the Atlantic Ocean.

Carlyle Hotel—PAST. Architects Richard Kiehnel and John Elliot designed the Streamline-styled Carlyle Hotel, located at 1250 Ocean Drive, in 1941. The Carlyle forms an impressive series of curves, vertical columns, and dramatic circular overhangs called eyebrows.

Carlyle Hotel—PRESENT. The Carlyle Hotel was painted buff and green on the inside and mauve on the outside. It was once a bustling hotel and later it harbored offices and a top-notch restaurant. The Carlyle was in the 1996 movie "The Birdcage" that starred Robin Williams, Gene Hackman, and Nathan Lane. The owners replaced the neon Carlyle sign with a Birdcage sign and refurbished the hotel for filming. It is now an apartment complex.

Clevelander Hotel—PAST. The fifty-room Clevelander Hotel, located at 1020 Ocean Drive, was designed by Albert Anis in 1937. It is best known for its poolside glass-block and neon bar.

Clevelander Hotel—PRESENT. The outdoor bar at the Cleveland Hotel is a popular hangout. Most people come here for a view of the lovely pool deck, live music, and the lively scene. On the second floor is the Clevelander gym.

Colony Hotel—PAST. The fifty-room Colony Hotel, located at 736 Ocean Drive, was designed by architect Henry Hohauser in 1935. The Colony marks the first time that the signage became part of the hotel. Neon outlined the lettering on a spire and canopy worthy of a 1930s movie palace.

Colony Hotel—PRESENT. The Colony is the oldest Art Deco hotel in Miami Beach. It is also probably the most photographed building in South Beach. Inside the lobby are excellent examples of space age interiors, including Saturn-shaped lamps and Flash Gordon elevators. A Ramon Chatov mural, featuring an agricultural scene, is above the green Vitrolite fireplace in the lobby.

Edison Hotel—PAST. The Mediterranean-styled Edison Hotel, located at 960 Ocean Drive, was designed by architect Henry Hohauser in 1935. The five-story, sixty-room hotel had an airy entrance arcade porch and a swimming pool tucked in back.

Edison Hotel—PRESENT. In 2009, Edison Hotel was closed and being renovated, possibly for use as a future condominium or apartment building. However, two sidewalk restaurants were still busy serving customers.

Leslie Hotel—PAST. Advertised as the beautiful ultra-modern building with cheerful rooms, the 43-room Leslie Hotel, located at 1244 Ocean Drive, was designed by architect Albert Anis and built in 1937.

Leslie Hotel—PRESENT. The Leslie Hotel was redone inside and out in a brilliant mix of tropical colors and the rooms featured a variety of decors and extras. The Leslie was one of the first hotels on Ocean Drive to be restored to its original condition. For awhile this lemon yellow, with handsome fluted column, hotel housed the Art Deco Welcome Center, operated by the Miami Design Preservation League, the non-profit preservation group responsible for the movement to preserve the Art Deco properties and listing them on the National Register of Historic Places. In late 2009, the hotel was closed with a "FOR SALE" sign in the window.

Park Central Hotel—PAST. The seven-story Park Central Hotel, located at 640 Ocean Drive, was designed by Henry Hohauser in 1937. This Mediterranean Revival style structure has a fluted eave, octagonal windows, and corners feathered by wraparound windows, giving it to float seven stories above a columned porch. The blue-and-white Art Deco beauty has a rooftop sundeck.

Park Central Hotel—PRESENT. The Park Central Hotel evokes a real sense of the area's past. An Art Deco favorite, this 1937 modern palace has terrazzo floors and wrought-iron stairwells throughout the lobby. Rooms feature mahogany ceiling fans, restored 1930s furniture, and spotless white walls. The hotel was temporarily modified as an old dilapidated rundown hotel to film "The Crew" starring Burt Reynolds and Richard Dreyfuss.

Tides Hotel—PAST. The 112-room Tides Hotel, located at 1220 Ocean Drive, was designed by architect L. Murray Dixon in 1936. It has porthole windows, abundant stainless steel, and ocean liner curves. The Tides' wide stair entry set a dramatic stage. Miami Beach was declining in the 1960s, and entertainers often had to work lobby shows at some of the small old hotels in South Beach. In the showroom at the Tides, entertainers had to bring their own piano player if they wanted music. In 1976, prices for overnight accommodations on South Beach were as low a $5 a night.

Tides Hotel—PRESENT. In the renovated Tides Hotel, the original 112 rooms were converted into forty-five 1930s-style suites that face the ocean head-on, with a 3,200-square-foot penthouse that has panoramic views in every direction. The hotel now has a terrazzo-floored restaurant and bar, and serves breakfast on the front terrace. Today, upscale hotels, like Tides, charge up to $5,000 for a luxury suite.

Waldorf Towers Hotel—PAST. The forty-room Waldorf Towers Hotel, located at 820 Ocean Drive, was designed by architect Albert Anis in 1937. The hotel has a cylindrical lighthouse tower that looks out to sea from atop its rounded rooftop corner.

Waldorf Towers Hotel—PRESENT. The renovated Waldorf Towers Hotel is now a yellow, purple, and white Art Deco gem with a bright tile veranda. It is a small, cool hotel in the heart of the popular South Beach area. It has a terrace restaurant that overlooks Ocean Drive.

White House Hotel—PAST.
The White House Hotel, located at 1455 Ocean Drive, was torn down.

Il Villago—PRESENT.
Now, the ultra-modern Il Villago anchors the north end of Ocean Drive.

Hotels Along Collins Avenue

National Hotel—PAST. Located at 1677 Collins Avenue, the National Hotel was designed by Roy F. France in 1939. The Streamline Moderne hotel was only one block from Lincoln Road and the Miami Beach Golf Course. It has 160-rooms, a 205-foot-long swimming pool framed by rows of palms, and the sculptural roof tower that crowns the hotel is a silver cupola over Moorish arches.

National Hotel—PRESENT. During World War II, the Army Air Corps moved its Miami Beach headquarters into National Hotel where sentinels kept a watch for German submarines from its tower. The hotel was renovated in 1996. The interior now takes you back to the grandness of the Art Deco era.

Ritz Plaza Hotel—PAST.

Ritz Plaza Hotel—PRESENT.

Located at 1701 Collins Avenue, on the outer fringe of the Art Deco District, this 132-room Streamline Moderne/Modern hotel was designed by architect L. Murray Dixon in 1940. It was formerly named the Grossinger until that famous Catskills resort family objected. The structure has rounded corners on projecting walls around the swimming pool and a sculptural roof tower that crowns the hotel. In 2009, the Ritz Plaza was closed and undergoing renovation.

Raleigh Hotel—PAST. The 110-room Raleigh Hotel is one of Miami Beach's Art Deco gems. Designed by noted architect Lawrence Murray Dixon, the hotel opened in 1940. At the white-tie ball on the hotel's opening night, an unknown Desi Arnaz was discovered when he filled in for a sick band member. Esther Williams filmed many of her famous swimming scenes in the Raleigh's curvaceous pool. *Life* magazine (the king of magazines in 1947) called the Raleigh's swimming pool "the most beautiful pool in the world."

Raleigh Hotel—PRESENT. Esther Williams doesn't perform aquatic routines for her movies in Raleigh's pool anymore, but between rounds of martinis, the poolside of the pineapple-shaped pool is a popular hangout for locals. The elaborate pool has been renovated to its former glory. The front of this Art Deco gem is partially hidden by a garden of tropical plants and palms. Decorated in a casual island style, the rooms are cool, charming, and contain elegant modern wrought iron furnishing. The Raleigh poolside is a place where everyone — from Calvin Klein to Johnny Depp and Kate Moss — is often seen.

Richmond Hotel—PAST.

Richmond Hotel—PRESENT.

The 105-room Modern style Richmond Hotel is located at 1757 Collins Avenue. It was designed by architect L. Murray Dixon in 1941. Today the front of the Richmond Hotel is almost completely hidden by tall palm trees.

Royal Palm Hotel—PAST. The Royal Palm Hotel, located at 1545 Collins Avenue, was built by Donald Smith in 1939. The hotel boasted a shower, bath, telephone, and radio in every room and in the late 1940s summer rates of $1.25 per day, including continental breakfast. Shown is the front cover of the hotel's matchbook.

Royal Palm Hotel—PRESENT. In 1987, Arthur Unger, grandson of the original owner, and his wife brought the hotel, which was now in a rundown condition, back to life. An airbrushed mural was exhumed from beneath old wallpaper. From under the Formica on the front desk they excavated marble and neon. The exterior was given a fresh coat of pink paint. Today, there is no better place to feel a sense of sea-borne movement than the Titanic-esque ocean-liner back lobby of this massive, beautifully restored hotel.

Shelborne Hotel—PAST. The fourteen-story, 150-room, $350,000 Shelborne Hotel, located at 1801 Collins Avenue, was designed by the architectural firm of Igor B. Polevitsky and Thomas Russell in 1940. The severe geometry of the horizontal window band and the vertical wall planes is relieved by the impressive signage on the roof-line.

Shelborne Hotel—PRESENT. This hotel has gone through several owners and considerable physical changes through the years. Hotel rooms were converted into 225 condo units, most of which are also rented as hotel rooms.

Shore Club Hotel—PAST.

Shore Club Hotel—PRESENT.

Located at 1901 Collins Avenue, the Shore Club resort is a large beachfront area with elaborate facilities for day and night relaxation on the shore. Brightly awninged cabanas were placed at right angles to the ten-mile private beach. A swimming pool separates the cabanas and sun terrace from the dining terrace and outdoor dancing pavilions. The 325-room hotel, built in 1939 as an integral part of the Shore Club Plan, was spacious, smart, and modern. Centrally located, it was headquarters for the area's liveliest social activity. If tourists didn't like ocean bathing, there were always pools like the one here at the Shore Club. And if the tourist didn't like pools either, there were always the girls and palm trees. Today the Shore Club is a luxury hotel with classy rooms and the exclusive Moroccan-themed Skybar.

St. Moritz Hotel—PAST. The ten-story St. Moritz Hotel, designed by architect Roy F. France in 1939, was located at 1601 Collins Avenue.

Loew's Miami Beach Hotel—PRESENT. In 1998, the seventeen-story Lowe's Hotel incorporated the historic Art Deco St. Moritz Hotel into the 780-room convention hotel's design.

Tiffany Hotel—PAST. The 53-room Tiffany Hotel, located at 801 Collins Avenue, was designed by architect L. Murray Dixon in 1939. Dixon designed a curved metal finial, a pointed ornament, on top of the hotel's masthead, which in turn sits on a futuristic finned cylinder. The futuristic architecture of the 1939 New York World's Fair influenced its design. Even though the hotel is a block off Ocean Drive, the rooftop octagonal pool deck offered a view of the Atlantic Ocean. During World War II, the hotel was used as barracks for Army Air Corp troops.

The Hotel—PRESENT. The Tiffany Hotel changed its name to "The Hotel" to settle a trademark dispute with the famed New York jewelry store. They were, however, allowed to keep the vertical TIFFANY sign. The lobby and patio areas of the Art Deco hotel are a salute to color, exuberance, and plain fabulousness.

Albion Hotel—PAST. The Albion Hotel, located at 1650 James Avenue, was designed by Igor Polevitsky in 1939. This Streamlined nautical design Art Deco 115-room hotel was advertised as the "hotel of tomorrow." At its front door is the world famous Lincoln Road shopping district; at the rear, the Miami Beach Municipal golf course. Luxurious rooms, suites, penthouse apartments, radios, solarium, steam heat, and air-conditioned dining room, as advertised in a 1941 magazine ad.

Albion Hotel—PRESENT. The Albion Hotel still sports the best in ocean liner imagery. Portholes puncture the side of the building and the setback upper story, now filled in, at one time had a ship's railing. Furthering the metaphor of the high seas, the crowning ornament on the top of the hotel offers the appearance of a ship's exhaust stack. This Art Deco hotel is now the nicest hotel on Lincoln Road Mall. The renovated hotel has a bit of color in the white-and-stainless-steel rooms.

Blackstone Hotel—PAST. The fourteen-story, Blackstone Hotel, located at 801 Washington Avenue, was designed by Kingstone Hall in 1929, and remodeled by V. H. Nellenbogen in 1934. This Mediterranean Eclectic hotel, the first Jewish hotel in Miami Beach, was noted for its clock on the rooftop.

Blackstone Hotel—PRESENT. In 1954, an African American Methodist church group was planning to hold a convention at the Blackstone Hotel. There were bomb threats from the Ku Klux Klan and even the synagogues were placed on alert. Today, the Blackstone structure, practically hidden by tall palm trees, still exists, but it is no longer a hotel.

Clay Hotel—PAST. Located at 1438 Washington Avenue, on the corner of Washington Avenue and Espanola Way, the Clay Hotel was a popular nightspot during the 1930s. This Mediterranean-style building was formerly the headquarters of mobster Al Capone's gambling syndicate. Capone's gambling casino was located on the second floor. Later, it was here that Cuban band leader Desi Arnaz helped create the rumba craze that spread across the country. Arnaz is perhaps better remembered as the real-life husband of comedienne Lucille Ball and her partner in the "I Love Lucy" television series.

Clay Hotel—PRESENT. With its wrought-iron balconies, the Clay Hotel has an Alpine look. It became a flophouse in the 1970s and housed Cuban refugees in 1980. Don Johnson, Elton John, and Sylvester Stallone have experienced the special atmosphere, as they filmed their movies and music videos here. The hotel's most important guests, however, continue to be the visitors who come from all over the world to experience the international allure of the hotel's Old World ambiance and the sultry tropical image of South Beach. Today the facility operated as a hostel and full-service hotel. It was the area's first youth hotel.

Kenmore Hotel—PAST.

Bel Aire Hotel—PRESENT.

The sixty-room Kenmore Hotel, located at 1050 Washington Avenue, was designed by architect Anton Skislewiczs. The hotel has a large lobby with a sweeping interior neon design. The Kenmore later became the Bel Aire Hotel, which has a small swimming pool and pool deck just outside its front entrance.

Nautilus Hotel—PAST. Carl G. Fisher, Miami Beach's greatest early developer, built the six-story Nautilus Hotel on twenty-five acres of tropical grounds overlooking Biscayne Bay. This luxury hotel, with Spanish decorative elements, was designed by New York architects Leonard Schultz and S. Fullerton Weaver in 1934. Fisher introduced polo to Miami Beach and built a polo field at the Nautilus. He also imported polo players from Europe to show "the locals" how the game was played. While visiting Italy, Jane Fisher sent her husband Carl a gondola from Venice, giving him the idea to spend $4,000 having his boat builders make copies. Soon Nautilus Hotel guests were enjoying piloted journeys on the Biscayne Bay.

Mount Sinai Hospital—PRESENT. During World War II, Nautilus Hotel was converted to an Army hospital. In 1949, the vacated Nautilus Hotel became Mount Sinai Hospital. In 1968, the Nautilus structure was demolished to make way for a new nursing school and pharmaceutical building for the Mount Sinai Medical Center.

Part IV: Coral Gables Past and Present

Chapter Fifteen: City Scenes

To the south and southwest of the City of Miami, one encounters the infinitely charming community of Coral Gables, one of the few local communities launched before the boom years of the 1920s. In 1898, the Rev. Solomon G. Merrick, a Congregational minister of Cap Cod, came to the area with his family to escape the icy northern winters. Afflicted with ill health, he decided to remain here in this incomparable climate and establish a fruit grove. Merrick bought a 160-acre tract here because of the high land, and the rich and fertile soil underlay with solid coral. His health improved greatly and he planned to establish a professional colony of small land tracts. Carrying on the work he had started, his son, George E. Merrick, conceived the idea of building a luxurious modern city. By 1921, George's holdings had expanded to 3,000 acres.

George Merrick's task was not easy; friends tried to discourage him, begging him to scrap his Utopia ideas. Merrick was not discouraged. He proceeded to build his dream into a reality, even insisting on a certain type of architecture — Mediterranean style, a combination of Italian and Spanish. An April 29, 1925, Coral Gables was incorporated. It was a beautiful suburban city, however, easily accessible to metropolitan Miami.

Many Miami leaders in financial, business, professional, and social affairs make their homes here, together with a large permanent number of families from throughout America. Coral Gables is a city of beautiful homes half-hidden by vines and fragrant flowering shrubbery, wide boulevards, plazas with seductive Spanish names, entrance gateways constructed of native rock and built by imported Spanish masons, buildings topped with copies of famous towers of Spain, schools, cathedral-like churches, bathing beaches with south sea glamour, thousands of transplanted tropical trees and plants thriving as in their native habitat. George Merrick's dream came true.

Coral Gables is unique among American cities inasmuch as it was already planned before the first construction was started. In the main portion, rigid restrictions limit building construction to the Mediterranean and Spanish style of rock, stucco, tile or concrete block, reinforced with steel. In the outlying sections are small areas restricted to Colonial, French, Dutch South African and Chinese style homes.

Though George Merrick did not name the "Miracle Mile," his original plans envisioned that fine shops along this broad, beautifully-landscaped thoroughfare in Coral Gables would one day attract visitors and residents from all over South Florida — as it certainly does today. This serene, sophisticated and completely self-contained community is also the seat of the University of Miami. Its big campus, set with striking ultramodern buildings, fills the southern half of Coral Gables and spreads into South Miami. Yet, predominantly, Coral Gables remains most notable for its innate charm and unspoiled character.

The fact that the University of Miami is located here is probably responsible for Coral Gables' sometimes startling contrasts. The University acts as a stimulus both physical and mental. Youthful vigor and exuberance is coupled with an extraordinary active culture life, making the city of many golf courses, swimming pools and beautiful beaches also the acknowledged cultural center of this part of Florida.

Coral Gables House—PAST. The house located at 907 Coral Way, was the George E. Merrick House, built about 1906 at the heart of the 160-acre citrus and vegetable farm developed by George's father, Congregational minister Rev. Solomon G. Merrick. After cultivating the farm, the Merricks became the largest exporters of grapefruit in the Southeast. The house, designed by George's mother Althea, was built of a local fossil-bearing limestone the Merricks mistook for coral and a gabled roof. The City of Coral Gables took its name from the Merrick House. The house shows an adaptation of classical New England style to a new climate and a new set of building materials. The house was raised above ground to allow cross ventilation and to protect it from flooding. Its steeply pitched, gabled roof featured a coral-colored tile. George, the city's founder, spent his childhood in this house before striking out to create Coral Gables — Miami's master suburb.

Coral Gables House—PRESENT. Gradually the house fell into disrepair and in 1976 became the property of the City of Coral Gables. The house was restored, decorated with period furnishings from the 1920s, and renamed the Coral Gables House. Some of the furnishings belonged to the Merrick family, including the baby grand piano, and the dining room and bedroom sets. Today the Coral Gables House is operated as a house museum open to the public for tours and meetings, and is listed on the National Register of Historic Places.

Coral Gables City Hall—PAST. The City Hall, located at 405 Biltmore Way, opened in early 1928. It was designed by architects Phineas Paist and Harold Steward and anchors the street known as the Miracle Mile, home of a fabulous shopping area. A dominating feature of the Key Largo limestone City Hall is the campanile, or square bell tower, and bronze belfry modeled after the municipal building in Seville, Spain, and William Strickland's nineteenth century Philadelphia Exchange Building. The tall columns in the curved portico reflect the Venetian influence and the rounded front is Italian in nature. Native stone is used throughout the building. The tiles on the roof were obtained in Cuba and Spain.

Coral Gables City Hall—PRESENT. Viewing the City Hall's integrated circular and square design, most impressive is a rounded wing with ornate columns and grotesque carvings true to the Mannerist style. The twelve columns fronting a semicircular rotunda is topped by a three-tier clock tower. Inside, items from Coral Gables' history line narrow corridors while the interior of the dome carries a Four Seasons mural by Denman Fink, an artist who worked closely with George Merrick. The structure has a coral rock facing on the base of the building. In May 2006, the Coral Gables Garden Club erected a statue of George Merrick in front of City Hall, the last building that he oversaw the design and construction of.

The Grand Hotel of Coral Gables—PAST. The Biltmore Hotel, located at Anastasia Avenue and Columbus Boulevard, a massive tile-roofed concrete structure with rambling wings and a lofty central tower designed in the Mediterranean style, dominated the Coral Gables landscape. The hotel served as headquarters to both sports and fashion. Throughout its years, the resort played host to European royalty, such as the Duke and Duchess of Windsor; Hollywood stars such as Judy Garland, Ginger Rogers, Bing Crosby, Dorothy Lamour, Tom Mix, Glenn Ford, Lucille Ball and Desi Arnaz, and Robert Redford; mobster Al Capone; President Bill Clinton; presidential families, the Carters and the Bushes; baseball great Babe Ruth; General Dwight D. Eisenhower; "Tarzan's" Johnny Weissmuller; and swimming star Esther Williams. Weissmuller broke a swimming record here. During the Depression, the Biltmore survived by throwing aquatic galas that drew large crowds.

The Grand Hotel of Coral Gables—PRESENT. The lobby of the Biltmore is grand, gorgeous, yet surprisingly not gaudy; it is like a child's fantasy of an Arab castle crossed with a Mediterranean villa. The oldest hotel in Coral Gables, it features hand-painted high domed ceilings, exquisite carvings, and a majestic sixteen-story tower rising high above the hotel.

Biltmore Hotel's Early Years—PAST. It is easier to grasp the Moorish majesty of the most important landmark in Coral Gables when you know it was designed by architects Leonard Schultze and S. Fullerton Weaver of New York — the same architects who built the Waldorf-Astoria in New York City and the Breakers, the poshest hotel in Palm Beach. They borrowed the design for the hotel's 300-foot tower from Seville, Spain's 800-year-old Giralda bell tower. The Biltmore Hotel, which opened in 1926, was labeled the acme of hostelry and clubs. No detail was too small to ignore, nor was anything too expensive to consider. The marble came from Italy, the china from Tiffany's, the chandeliers were crystal, enormous fireplaces gave the impression of a lordly castle, and gold leaf on the ceilings sparkled in the firelight.

Biltmore Hotel's Later Years—PRESENT. For all its offerings to the wealthy, even the richest were unable to support the enormous cost of the hotel. In 1941, Biltmore Hotel was pressed into service and transformed into an Army-Air Force Regional Hospital. After World War II, the hospital continued to operate as a Veterans Administration Hospital until 1968. In 1973, the structure was turned over to the City of Coral Gables. In 1987, after $52 million in renovations and modernizations, it reopened as a luxury hotel. It closed again in 1990 and reopened in 1992 under the management of Westin Hotels and Resorts, and Seaway Hotels Corporation.

Biltmore Hotel, the Classiest Joint in Town—PAST. A service building and garage is at the far left. Tennis courts were located behind the service building. To the right of the garage was the three-story building used to house hotel employees. The Country Club complex is at the extreme right. On the 155-acre grounds were two 18-hole golf courses and a canal system that led to Tahiti Beach at Biscayne Bay and the ocean beyond.

Biltmore Hotel, the Classiest Joint in Town—PRESENT. The massive 286-room Biltmore Hotel, with its charm and sophistication, has endowed Coral Gables with an architectural landmark consistent with the Mediterranean-Revivalist style of homes in the surrounding area.

Biltmore Swimming Pool—PAST. The pool is the largest outdoor swimming pool in the continental United States. The 150 by 225-foot pool, which had a capacity of 1,250,000 gallons of water, provided a spectacular setting for water activities.

Biltmore Swimming Pool—PRESENT. One writer described the Biltmore's enormous pool as resembling a Sultan's water garden from "One Thousand & One Nights." The beautiful pool has survived the hotel's many changes of ownership, to the advantage of its modern-day guests.

University of Miami—PAST. The University of Miami was preparing to open in September 1926, but in mid-September of that year a hurricane roared up from the Caribbean to batter the surprised City of Miami and to slap Coral Gables a desperate blow. The University opened October 15, 1926, in the half finished bankrupt Anastasia Hotel building with wallboard partitions, thus earning the nickname "The Cardboard College." It opened, though, and stayed open through years when nothing was certain but debt. In 1940, there were 1,614 students enrolled. By 1967, all the activities in the old Anastasia Building had been transferred to the main campus and the building was demolished in 1968.

University of Miami—PRESENT. In the mid-1950s, the University of Miami began a massive building campaign. The original 160-acre campus was expanded to the present-day 245 acres. By the late 1960s the plans and dreams of the University's founders in 1926 had been exceeded and today the university is considered one of the nation's major universities. Shown is the School of Business Administration, originally built in 1980, with additions in 1995 and 2003. The campus consists of a repository of 1950s and 1960s architectural buildings and modern buildings in a botanical garden of stately royal palms, tropical shrubs and flowers, and winding shaded pathways.

Sevilla Hotel—PAST. The 27-room Mediterranean Revival style Sevilla Hotel, located at Ponce de Leon Boulevard and Alcazar Avenue, was built in 1926. It was furnished uniquely with antiques, lending a European elegance. It was originally designed by Anthony Zink as an office building and then later converted to a hotel.

Hotel Place St. Michel—PRESENT. The Sevilla Hotel, known as the King Richard Inn during the 1960s, underwent a major restoration in 1979 and became the quaint European-like Hotel Place de Michel. The building is noteworthy for its framed entrance on Alcazar Avenue and the arched windows on the first floor of street facades. The restaurant is a favorite for breakfast meetings and elegant dinners. Plenty of Old World charm here. All of the hotel rooms have different personalities, decorated with elegant antiques, buttery walls, windows that open and give visitors the appearance they are in Europe. The hotel is conveniently located only a block from Coral Gables' famed Miracle Mile shopping district.

Venetian Pool—PAST. The Venetian Pool was originally a quarry from which limestone, or coral rock, was taken for the construction of early Coral Gables homes. In 1924, Denman Fink, artist-architect and uncle of Coral Gables founder George Merrick, transformed it into a unique pool resembling a natural lagoon in a Venetian setting. His design included bridges, towers, a bathing casino, and lush landscaping. In the 1920s, the freshwater pool was used to promote Coral Gables and to highlight the city's distinctive architecture. William Jennings Bryan lectured here on the merits of living in Coral Gables. Annett Kellerman and Jackie Ott, the aqua tot, were among the famous visiting swimmers. Jan Garber, Paul Whiteman, and their orchestras played for social functions. In 1927, the pool was sold to the City of Coral Gables.

Venetian Pool—PRESENT. The Venetian Pool has been in operation as a public swimming pool continuously, except for a brief period in 1987 when the City of Coral Gables undertook a $2 million restoration that included a method to recycle the more than 820,000 gallons of water that it takes to fill the pool. It is one of the most beautiful and unique municipal swimming pools in the world. The Venetian Pool still remains a popular place, attracting some 1,400 people on a busy summer's day. That is quite a crowd, but it is a large pool (approximately 300-feet by 200-feet), one of the largest in the state. It is not the size that distinguishes this Coral Gables swimming pool, but its style. Visitors love swimming and sunbathing here, savoring the romantic flavor of days gone by.

DeSoto Plaza—PAST. Fourteen plazas were designed in Coral Gables by Denman Fink and landscaped by Frank M. Button. The first to be built in 1921 was the Ponce de Leon Plaza at Coral Way and Granada Boulevard. Shown is the DeSoto Plaza, an intersection that features a monumental freestanding fountain in the center. Located at Seville Avenue, Granada and DeSoto Boulevards, the fountain is a pedestal type that supports an obelisk and features relief carvings of four faces that each contain a fountain jet. The Biltmore Hotel is in the background.

DeSoto Plaza—PRESENT. The fountain at DeSoto Plaza is a favorite of visitors and natives alike. Water streams out of the mouths of carved faces into the fountain's large stone basin, and next to each face is an image of a three-masted ship. In this view is the tower of the Biltmore Hotel. A small parking lot at the fountain is used by visitors to the Venetian Pool.

Douglas Entrance to Coral Gables—PAST. The cohesive plan for Coral Gables was especially evident in the construction of the formal entrances to the city and the development of plazas to punctuate the network of streets that interlace it. Denman Fink, George Merrick's artistic advisor, designed eight major entrances for the city, but only four were completed. They were the Main or Douglas Entrance (Douglas Road and S.W. Eighth Street), the Commercial Entrance (Alhambra Circle and Douglas Road), the Granada Entrance (Tamiami Trail and Granada Boulevard) and the Country Club Prado Entrance (S.W. Eighth Street and the Country Club Prado). The massive arched portals, constructed of coral rock roofed with antique clay tiles, were like picture frames defining the vistas of the wide boulevards that pass through them.

Douglas Entrance to Coral Gables—PRESENT. The Douglas Entrance, designed and built at a cost of $1 million, is now surrounded by office buildings, creating a commercial use for the original ten-acre site, which was originally planned to be a Spanish village.

Granada Entrance—PAST. The Granada Entrance to Coral Gables, located at Granada Boulevard and Tamiami Trail (S.W. 8th Street), was constructed in 1922, the first of seven entrances planned for the city. Thought to be inspired by similar entrance gates in Spain, the 340-foot-long structure features a forty-foot arch that spans Granada Boulevard.

Granada Entrance—PRESENT. Today the Granada Entrance is on the opposite side of a busy intersection on the Tamiami Trail. A busy shopping center is located at the intersection.

Coral Gables Congregational Church—PAST. The Coral Gables Congregational Church, shown to the left of the Biltmore Hotel, was a Mediterranean-Revival structure that was built in 1924 on land donated by George Merrick. Some of the interior wood furnishings date from the sixteenth century and were recovered from shipwrecks. Some of the beams were deliberately aged to make the building look older. The church was inspired by a church in Barcelona, Spain. The Congregational Church, with its lovely baroque belfry and sculpture over the main entrance, was one of the community's earliest religious structures. It is located at 3010 DeSoto Boulevard.

Coral Gables Congregational Church—PRESENT. The Congregational Church was the first church built in Coral Gables. The church has retained both its superb exterior as well as its interior spaces. In addition to the church, architect Richard Kiehnel also designed the Seybold Building and the Scottish Rite Masonic Temple in downtown Miami. The church grounds are landscaped with stately palms and the interior is graced with its unaltered sanctuary, with its tile floors, polychromed beams and spindles. In addition to its impressive choirs, this church hosts various concert series, from classical to jazz, all of which draw regional crowds to it beautiful Mediterranean setting.

Coral Gables Country Club—PAST. The Coral Gables Country Club, opened in 1923 at 997 North Greenway Drive, overlooked the nine-hole, 58-acre Granada Golf Course where diners could leisurely watch the play. The club was built of coral rock in the heart of a residential area. Its three stage tower was the focal point of the design and provided the main entry to the building. The Country Club dining room could accommodate five hundred diners. In the 1920s dinner prices were $1.50 and $2.00; ale, 5 cents; and ice, 25 cents. The club had an open air dance floor. Lights were hung amidst a grove fo mature coconut palms to illuminate the gleaming terrazzo dance floor. Admission per couple was $1. Orchestras led by Jan Garber and Paul Whiteman played at the club.

Coral Gables Country Club—PRESENT. Almost all of the original Country Club building was destroyed by a devastating fire in 1983. The tower, however, was reconstructed.

Tropical Park Race Course—PAST. Miami's season of sports revolved around the race horse, the racing greyhound, and Jai-Alai. Owners, trainers, touts, and hangers-on filled the hotels and rooming houses in the area. The paddocks and grandstand at Tropical Park swarmed with eager humanity each afternoon. Located one and a half miles west of Coral Gables on Bird Road, Tropical Park ran its first horse race on December 26, 1931. In 1932 the Grandstand was modified and the surrounding area landscaped. Al Capone and his men, moved into the Miami area in a big way and controlled the races at Tropical Park. Miami was ashamed of the hoodlums who were running Tropical Park and eventually forced the mobsters to sell their ownership in the race track to honest men.

Equestrian Center—PRESENT. The Tropical Park Race Course continued to operate until 1972. It was purchased by Churchill Downs in 1998 and today Tropical Park operates as an Equestrian Center that hosts thirty or more horse shows annually. Visitors can also enjoy bicycling, walking or running on the miles of beautifully landscaped pathways.

Miracle Mile—PAST. Coral Way (S.W. 24th Street), is the major east-west street through Coral Gables. The section that runs down the central business district, from S.W. 37th to 42nd avenues (Douglas to LeJeune Road), is known as Miracle Mile, an area of swanky shops and brick-lined streets. Shown are partial views of the F. W. Woolworth Company (on the left) and the 1926 Colonnade Building (on the right).

Miracle Mile—PRESENT. Today, Miracle Mile has planted landscaping in the median of Coral Way. The F. W. Woolworth Company building is now a Barnes & Noble Bookstore and the original sales office for George Merrick's Coral Gable Corporation, the Colonnade Building, is now a greatly enlarged high-rise hotel and office building. Over the years the Colonnade Building has housed many businesses, including a First National Bank of Coral Gables, a motion picture studio in 1940, and a World War II pilot training center and parachute factory. The Colonnade Hotel incorporates its original Spanish Renaissance façade and a two-story, marble-floored rotunda with a late nineteenth century décor and European elegance. Luxurious details in its 157 rooms and suites include carved mahogany furniture, marble vanities, and gold bathroom fixtures.

Fairchild Tropical Garden—PAST. The Fairchild Tropical Garden is located at 10901 Old Cutler Road, ten miles southwest of the center of Miami. It is one of the world's premier tropical botanical gardens, with eighty-three acres of palms, flowering trees, flowering vines, ferns, bamboos, orchids and bromeliads. The collection of some five hundred species of palms is generally recognized as the most important documented palm collection in the world. The garden was started in 1938 by Colonel Robert H. Montgomery, an avid plant collector. Colonel Montgomery was encouraged and aided by his close friend Dr. David Fairchild, for whom the garden was later named. Dr. Fairchild was one of the most noted and respected American plant explorers of his time and enjoyed worldwide recognition as a botanist. As the head of the U.S. Department of Agriculture "Seed and Plant Introduction Section," he introduced more than 2,000 varieties of trees, plants, fruit, vegetables and grains into this country.

Fairchild Tropical Garden—PRESENT. Fairchild Tropical Garden has over 5,000 types of plants and is one of South Florida's natural treasures. A world-renowned legacy of research, education and conservation distinguishes the garden. Over the years, Fairchild scientists have worked to increase and deepen our knowledge and conservation of plants. Countless palms, miles of winding paths, acres of sapphire blue lakes, spectacular flowering trees and vines, all kinds of bromeliads, a rainforest, a profusion of ferns, beautiful ponds, birds, alligators, a butterfly garden, and endless perfect views. The 83-acre garden is divided into several regions. A 16,428-square-foot conservatory featuring rare orchids, aroids, bromeliads, and fruit trees; the McLamore Arboretum, which displays more than 740 species of tropical flowering trees on eight acres; the world-renowned Montgomery Palmetum, with an impressive selection of palms from around the world; the William F. Whitman Tropical Fruit Pavilion, which features a 38-foot-high pavilion where visitors can view exotic tropical fruit species form areas such as the Amazon and Borneo; and the Keys Coastal Habitat which attracts migratory birds and Florida fauna with plants native to South Florida and the Florida Keys.

Suggested Readings

The following is a list of books that will give you a better understanding of the Greater Miami area.

Allman, T. D. *Miami: City of the Future*. New York, New York: Atlantic Monthly Press, 1987.

Armbruster, Ann. *The Life and Times of Miami Beach*. New York, New York: Alfred A. Knopf, 1995.

Arnold, Kathy and Paul Wade. *Florida*. Washington, D. C.: National Geographic Society, 1999.

Ayers, R. Wayne. *Florida's Grand Hotels from the Gilded Age*. Charleston, South Carolina: Arcadia Publishing, 2005.

Beach, Rex. *The Miracle of Coral Gables*. Coral Gables, Florida: George Edgar Merrick, 1926.

Beebe, Morton. *Miami: The Sophisticated Tropics*. San Francisco, California: Chronicle Books, 1991.

Biondi, Joanne. *Miami Beach Memories*. Guilford, Connecticut: The Globe Pequot Press, 2007.

Biondi, Joann, editor. *Miami*. London, England: Apa Publications, Ltd., 1996.

Biondi, Joann and Tony Arruza. *Miami: A City Life Pictorial Guide*. Stillwater, Minnesota: Voyageur Press, 2000.

Blackman, E. V. *Miami and Dade County, Florida*. Washington, D. C.: Victor Rainbolt, 1921.

Blank, Joan Gill. *Key Biscayne: A History of Miami's Tropical Island and the Cape Florida Lighthouse*. Sarasota, Florida: Pineapple Press, Inc., 1996.

Braden, Susan R. *The Architecture of Leisure*. Gainesville, Florida: University Press of Florida, 2002.

Bramson, Seth H. *Florida East Coast Railway*. Charleston, South Carolina: Arcadia Publishing, 2006.

From Sandbar to Sophistication: The Story of Sunny Isles Beach. Charleston, South Carolina: The History Press, 2007.

Hialeah, Miami Springs & Opa Locka. Charleston, South Carolina: The History Press, 2008.

L'chaim! The History of the Jewish Community of Greater Miami. Charleston, South Carolina: The History Press, 2008.

Miami Beach. Charleston, South Carolina: Arcadia Publishing, 2005.

Brown, Warren J. *Florida's Aviation History*. Largo, Florida: Aero-Medical Consultants, Inc., 1994.

Bullen, Adelaide K. *Florida Indians of Past and Present*. Gainesville, Florida: Kendall Books, 1965.

Butko, Briam and Sarah Butko. *Roadside Attractions*. Mechanicsburg, Pennsylvania: Stackpole Books, 2007.

Calson, Charlie. *Weird Florida*. New York, New York: Barnes & Noble Publishing, 2005.

Carr, Robert S. and John Ricisak. *The Miami Circle*. Tallahassee, Florida: Florida Anthropological Society, 2000.

Cerwinske, Laura. *Tropical Deco: The Architecture and Design of Old Miami Beach*. New York, New York: Rizzoli International Publications, 1981.

Chasan, Gail, editor. *Fodor's Greater Miami and the Gold Coast*. New York, New York: Fodor's Travel guides, 1987.

Chase, Iris Garnett and Gabriele Schuetz. *South Beach Faces & Facades*. Atglen, Pennsylvania: Schiffer Publishing, Ltd., 2007

Chase, Iris Garnett and Susan Russell. *South Beach Deco: Step by Step*. Atglen, Pennsylvania: Schiffer Publishing Ltd., 2005.

Clarke, Mary Helm. *South Florida Treasure Trails*. Tallahassee, Florida: Kay Publishing Company, 1949.

Clemence, Paul. *South Beach Architectural Photographs: Art Deco to Contemporary*. Atglen, Pennsylvania: Schiffer Publishing Ltd., 2006.

Congdon-Martin, Douglas. *South Beach Perspectives*. Atglen, Pennsylvania: Schiffer Publishing Ltd., 2007.

Corey, Sandler. *Miami with Fort Lauderdale and Key West*. New York, New York: McGraw-Hill, 2001.

Crittenden, John. *Hialeah Park: A Racing Legend*. Miami, Florida: Pickering Press, 1989.

Cummings, Susanne and Stuart Cummings. *Florida: Sights and Scenes of Miami*. Houston, Texas: Gulf Publishing Company, 1995.

Didion, Joan. *Miami*. New York, New York: Simon and Schuster, 1987.

Dunlop, Beth and Roberto Schezen. *Miami Trends and Traditions*. New York, New York: Monacelli Press, 1996.

Dunn, Hampton. *Re-Discover Florida*. Tampa, Florida: Trend House, 1969.

Federal Writers' Project. *Florida: A Guide to the Southernmost State*. New York, New York: Oxford University Press, 1939.

Fischer, Marsha. *Miami*. Minneapolis, Minnesota: Dillon Press, 1990.

Fisher, Jane. *Fabulous Hoosier*. Chicago, Illinois: Harry Coleman & Company, 1953.

Fox, Debbie and Marie-Helene Paquette Suarez. *Sharing the Sun*. Miami, Florida: Valiant Press, 1996.

Frazure, Hoyt. *Memories of Old Miami*. Miami, Florida: The Miami Herald.

Friend, Sandra and Kathy Wolf. *An Explorer's Guide: South Florida*. Woodstock, Vermont: The Countryman Press, 2006.

Gaby, Donald C. *An Historical Guide to the Miami River and Its Tributaries*. Miami, Florida: Historical Association of southern Florida, 1990.

The Miami River and Its Tributaries. Miami, Florida: The Historical Association of Southern Florida, 1993.

Gaines, Steven. *Fools Paradise*. New York, New York: Crown Publishers, 2009.

George, Paul S. *The Dr. Paul George Walking Tour of East Little Havana*. Miami, Florida: Historical Association of Southern Florida, 1991.

Gilbert, John W. *Miami and The Keys*. Florence, Italy: Casa Editrice Bonechi, 1992.

Gittner, Cory H. *Miami's Parrot Jungle and Gardens*. Gainesville, Florida: University Press of Florida, 2000.

Gross, Steve and Sue Daley. *Old Florida: Florida's Magnificent Homes, Gardens, and Vintage Attractions*. New York, New York: Rizzoli International Publications, 2003.

Harper, George Ro. *Making Golf History in South Florida*. Miami, Florida: Historical Association of Southern Florida.

Hiaasen, Carl. *Kick Ass*. Gainesville, Florida: University Press of Florida, 1999.

Hollingsworth, Tracy. *History of Dade County, Florida*. Self-published, 1936.

Howard, Craig and Cheri Howard. *Miami*. Key West, Florida: Self-published, 2004.

Humphreys, Andrew, editor. *Time Out Miami*. London, England: Time Out Guides Limited, 2004.

Hurley, Neil E. *An Illustrated History of Cape Florida Lighthouse*. Camino, California: Historic Lighthouse Publishers, 1989.

Karlin, Adam. *Miami & The Keys*. Oakland, California: Lonely Planet Publications, 2008.

Kearney, Bob, Editor. *Mostly Sunny Days*. Miami, Florida: Miami Herald Publishing Company, 1986.

Keel, James R. *Florida's Trails to History's Treasures*. Fort Lauderdale, Florida: Seajay Enterprises, Inc., 1981.

Kennedy, Patricia. *Miami Beach in Vintage Postcards*. Charleston, South Carolina: Arcadia Publishing, 2000.

Miami in Vintage Postcards. Charleston, South Carolina: Arcadia Publishing, 2000.

Kennedy, Stetson. *Palmetto Country*. Tallahassee, Florida: Florida A & M University Press, 1989.

Kleinberg, Eliot. *Weird Florida*. Marietta, Georgia: Longstreet, 1998.

Kleinberg, Howard. *Miami Beach: A History*. Miami, Florida: Centennial Press, 1994.

Miami: The Way We Were. Tampa, Florida: Surfside Publishing, 1989.

Woggles and Cheese Holes: The History of Miami Beach's Hotel. Miami Beach, Florida: The Grater Miami & The Beaches Hotel Association, 2005.

Kronstadt, Harold. *Views from the Beach*. Miami, Florida: Hallmark Press, 1987.

La Gorce, John Oliver. *Florida—The Fountain of Youth*. Washington, D. C.: National Geographic Society, Volume LVII, 1930.

LaRoue, Samuel D. Jr. and Ellen J. Uguccioni. *Coral Gables in Postcards: Scenes From Florida's Yesterday*. Miami, Florida: Dade Heritage Trust, 1988.

Lavender, Abraham D. *Miami Beach in 1920*. Charleston, South Carolina: Arcadia Publishing, 2002.

Leddick, David. *In the Spirit of Miami Beach*. New York, New York: Assouline Publishing, 2006.

Lee, Martin. *The Seminoles*. New York, New York: Franklin Watts, 1991.

Maltz, Alan S. and Les Standiford. *Miami: City of Dreams*. Key West, Florida: Light Flight Publications, 1997.

Martin, Mary, Tina Skinner and Nathaniel Wolfgang-Price. *Miami Memories: A Midcentury Journey*. Atglen, Pennsylvania: Schiffer Publishing Ltd., 2006.
McGoun, William E. *Ancient Miamians: The Tequesta of South Florida*. Gainesville, Florida: University Press of Florida, 2002.
Prehistoric Peoples of South Florida. Tuscaloosa, Alabama: The University of Alabama Press, 1993.
McIver, Stuart. *Glimpses of South Florida History*. Miami, Florida: Florida Flair Books, 1988.
Merrick Moments. Coral Gables, Florida: City of Coral Gables. 2000.
Miami: Garden City. New York, New York: Nelson Doubleday, Inc., 1966.
Miami and Dade County (American Guide Series). Northport, New York: Bacon, Percy & Daggett, publishers, 1941.
Miami The Beautiful. Miami, Florida: Foster & Reynolds Company, 1920.
Millas, Aristides J. and Ellen J. Uguccioni. *Coral Gables: Miami Riviera*. Miami, Florida: Dade Heritage Trust, 2003.
Mills, J. Calvin. *Highlights of Greater Miami*. Miami Shores, Florida: Mills Publications, 1952.
Morris, Theodore. *Florida's Lost Tribes*. Gainesville, Florida: University Press of Florida, 2004.
Moore, Marilyn A. *Access Miami*. New York, New York: HarperCollins Publishers, 1996.
Muir, Helen. *The Biltmore: Beacon for Miami*. Miami, Florida: Valiant Press, 1998.
Murrell, Muriel V. *Miami: A Backward Glance*. Sarasota, Florida: Pineapple Press, Inc., 2003.
Nash, Charles Edgar. *The Magic of Miami Beach*. Philadelphia, Pennsylvania: David McKay Company, 1938.
Olson, Arlene R. *A Guide to the Architecture of Miami Beach*. Dade Heritage Trust, Inc., 1978.
Parks, Arva Moore and Carolyn Klepper. *Miami Then and Now*. San Diego, California: Thunder Bay Press, 2002.
Parks, Arva Moore. *George Merrick's Coral Gables*. Miami, Florida: Ponce Circle Development LLC, 2006.
Miami Memories—John Sewell. Miami, Florida: Arva Parks & Co., 1987.
Miami: The Magic City. Tulsa, Oklahoma: Continental Heritage Press, 1981.
Miami Then & Now. Miami, Florida: Centennial Press, 1992.
The New Miami: The Magic City. Miami, Florida: Community Media, 2008.
Patricios, Nicholas N. *Building Marvelous Miami*. Gainesville, Florida: University Press of Florida, 1994.
Perez, Elizabeth P. *Florida Cuban Heritage Trail*. Tallahassee, Florida: Florida Department of State, 1994.
Pinkas, Lilly. *Guide to the Gardens of Florida*. Sarasota, Florida: Pineapple Press, 1998.
Plotner, Kevin and Rebecca Plotner. *Ocean Drive Guidebook: Ask A Local*. Atglen, Pennsylvania: Schiffer Publishing Ltd., 2008.
The Fontainebleau Miami. Atglen, Pennsylvania: Schiffer Publishing Ltd., 2008.
Walking Tour of Lincoln Road, South Beach. Atglen, Pennsylvania: Schiffer Publishing Ltd., 2007.
Pohlen, Jerome. *Oddball Florida*. Chicago, Illinois: Chicago Review Press, Inc., 2004.
Protko, Rhoda Ogden. *In and Around South Miami*. Miami, Florida: South Miami Area Chamber of Commerce, 1976.
Rieff, David. *Going to Miami*. Boston, Massachusetts: Little, Brown and Company, 1987.
Riley, Edward. *The Growth of Florida*. Edison, New Jersey: Chartwell Books, Inc., 2007.
Riley, Trish. *Palm Beach, Miami, and the Florida Keys*. Woodstock, Vermont: Countryman Press, 2005.
Rodriguez, Ivan A. and Margot Ammidown. *From Wilderness to Metropolis*. Miami, Florida: Metropolitan Dade County, 1992.
Roy, Joaquin. *The Streets of Coral Gables*. Coral Gables, Florida: University of Miami, 1989.
Russel, Susan. *South Beach Lifeguard Stations*. Atglen, Pennsylvania: Schiffer Publishing Ltd., 2008.
South Beach Postcards. Atglen, Pennsylvania: Schiffer Publishing, Ltd., 2007.
Sandler, Corey. *Miami*. New York, New York: McGraw-Hill, 2001.
Sinclair, Mick. *Drive Around Florida*. Peterbough, United Kingdom: Thomas Cook Publishing, 2005.
Smiley, Nixon. *Yesterday's Miami*. Miami, Florida: E.A. Seemann Publishing, 1973.
Smith, Mike. *South Florida Frontiers*. Miami, Florida: Florida Power & Light Company, 1957.
Spencer, Donald D. *Miami and Miami Beach in Early Postcards*. Ormond Beach, Florida: Camelot Publishing Company, 2002.

Spritzer, Lois. *Miami & Ft. Lauderdale*. New York, New York: Harper Collins Publisher, 1993.

Stanford, Emma. *Exploring Florida*. New York, New York: Foder's Travel Publications, 1993.

Stewart, Laura and Susanne Hupp. *Historic Homes of Florida*. Sarasota, Florida: Pineapple Press, Inc., 1995.

Stofik, M. Barron. *Saving South Beach*. Gainesville, Florida: University Press of Florida, 2005.

Trautman, James. *Pan American Clippers: The Golden Age of Flying Boats*. Ontario, Canada: Boston Mills Press, 2007.

Wheeler, Ryan J. and Robert Carr. *The Miami Circle*. Tallahassee, Florida: Florida Anthropological Society, 2004.

Wilpon, Bonnie. *Hollywood, Florida*. Charleston, South Carolina: Arcadia Publishing, 1999.

Wilson, F. Page. *Miami: From Frontier to Metropolis*. Miami, Florida: Historical Association of Southern Florida, 1954.

Wisser, Bill. *South Beach: America's Riviera, Miami Beach, Florida*. New York, New York: Arcade Publishing, 1995.

Work Projects Administration. *Going to Miami and Environs*. Northport, New York: Bacon, Percy & Daggett, 1941.

Index

MIAMI
florida